Collins
INTERNATIONAL
PRIMARY
MATHS

Workbook 1

William Collins' dream of knowledge for all began with the publication of his first book in 1819.
A self-educated mill worker, he not only enriched millions of lives, but also founded a flourishing publishing house. Today, staying true to this spirit, Collins books are packed with inspiration, innovation and practical expertise. They place you at the centre of a world of possibility and give you exactly what you need to explore it.

Collins. Freedom to teach.

An imprint of HarperCollins*Publishers*
The News Building
1 London Bridge Street
London
SE1 9GF

HarperCollins*Publishers*
1st Floor, Watermarque Building, Ringsend Road
Dublin 4, Ireland

Browse the complete Collins catalogue at
www.collins.co.uk

© HarperCollins*Publishers* Limited 2016

12

ISBN 978-0-00-815980-1

Lisa Jarmin and Ngaire Orsborn assert their moral rights to be identified as the authors of this work.

British Library Cataloguing in Publication Data
A catalogue record for this publication is available from the British Library.

Commissioned by Fiona McGlade
Series editor Peter Clarke
Project editor Kate Ellis
Project managed by Emily Hooton
Developed by Joan Miller and Tracy Thomas
Edited by Catherine Dakin
Proofread by Tanya Solomons
Answer check by Steven Matchett
Cover design by Ink Tank
Cover artwork by Rob Hainer/Shutterstock
Internal design by Ken Vail Graphic Design
Typesetting by Ken Vail Graphic Design
Illustrations by Ken Vail Graphic Design, Advocate Art and QBS
Production by Lauren Crisp
Printed and bound in the UK using 100% Renewable Electricity at CPI Group (UK) Ltd

Photo acknowledgements

Every effort has been made to trace copyright holders. Any omission will be rectified at the first opportunity.

Front cover and title page Rob Hainer/Shutterstock, p23t Shutterstock/La Gorda, p23 strawberries mart/ Shutterstock, p23 apples Jane Kelly/Shutterstock, p25 toys Matthew Cole/Shutterstock, p30 apples Jane Kelly/Shutterstock.

Contents

Measure

Handling data

The numbers 0 to 10

Trace

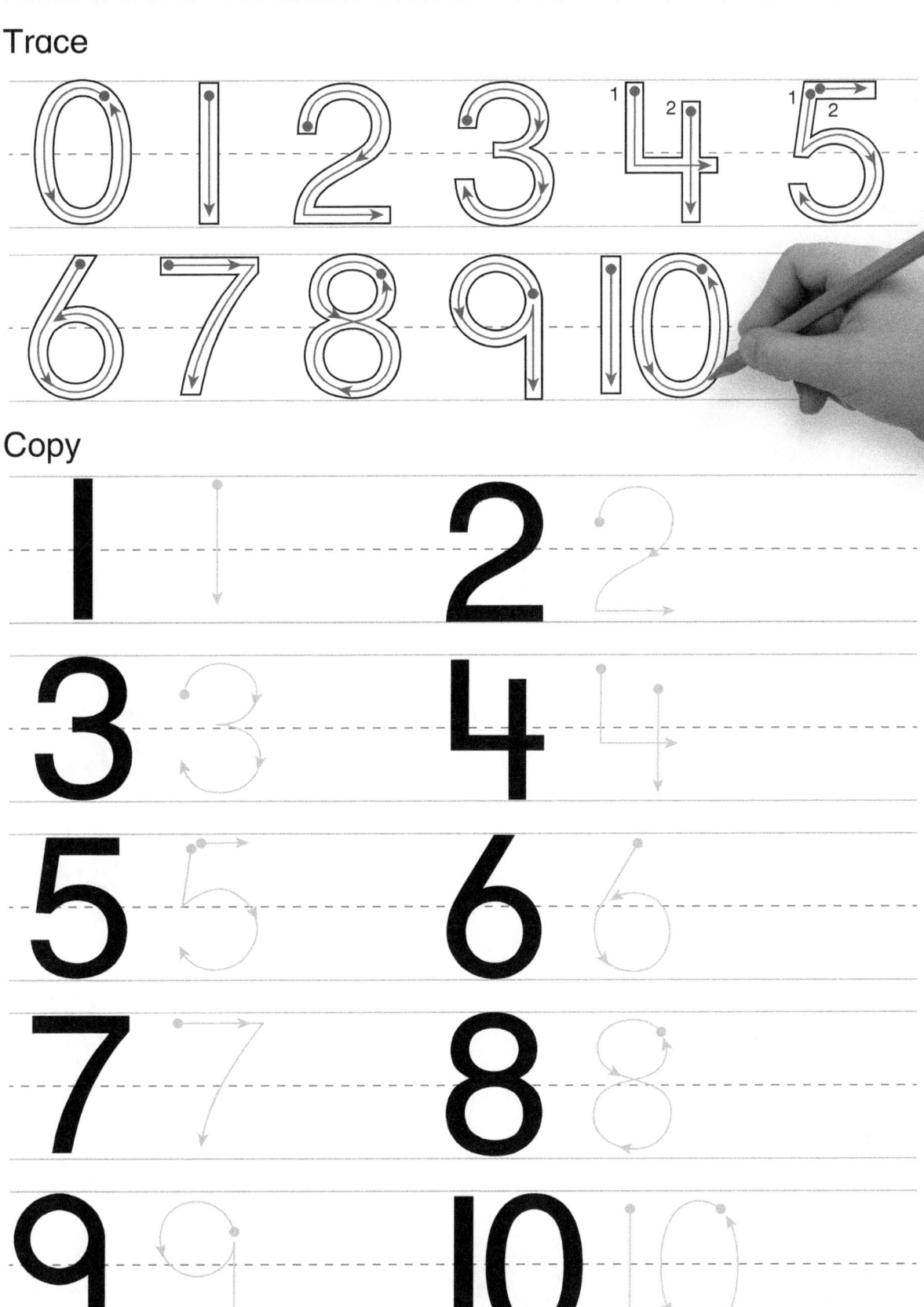

Copy

How many?

1

2

3

4

5

6

7

8

9

10

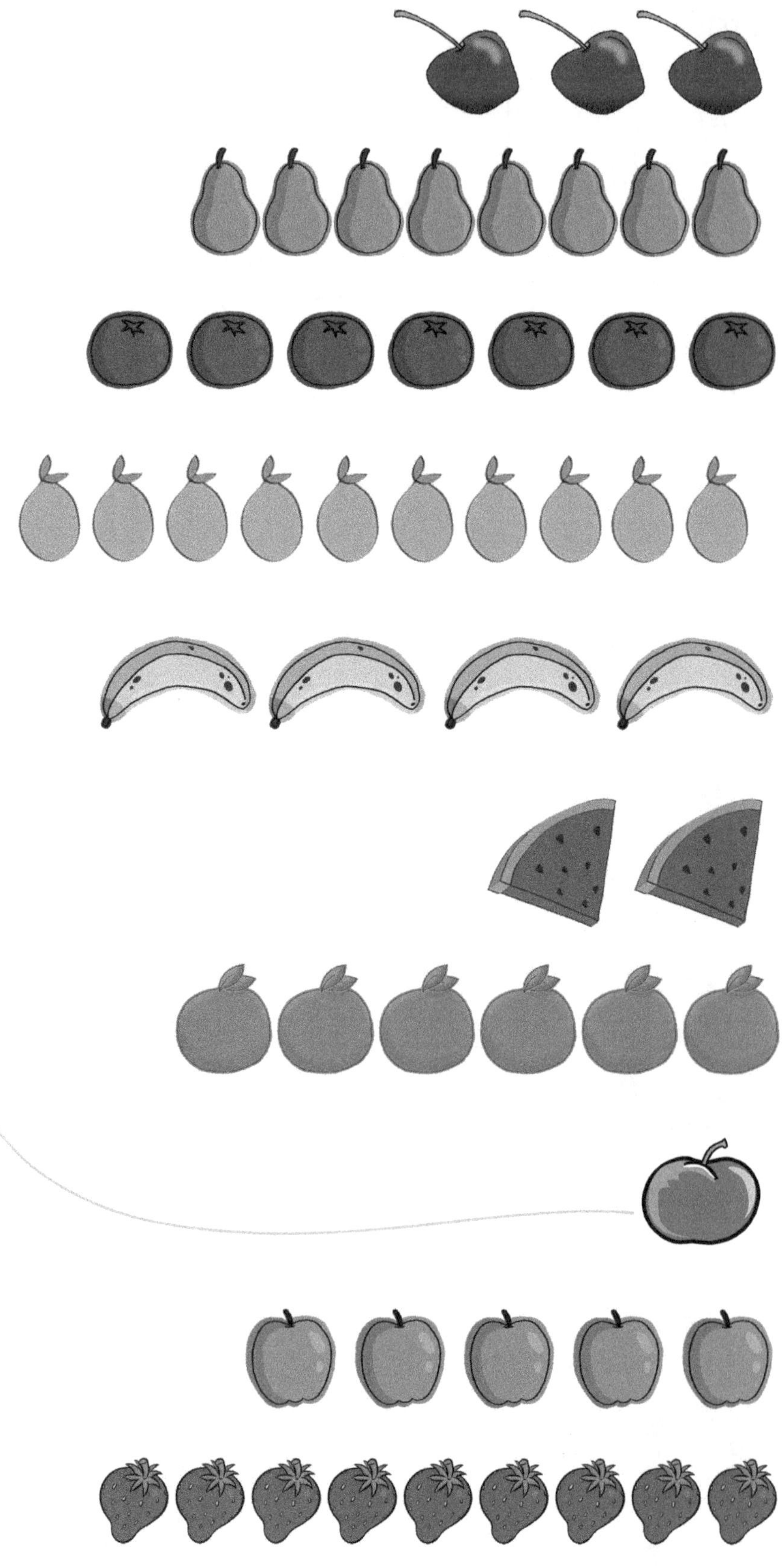

Lesson 1: **Counting in 1s**

- Count on in 1s from 0 to 100
- Count back in 1s from 20 to 0

Challenge 1 Trace the line and count on.

1, 2, 3, ...

Challenge 2 Trace the line and count back.

20, 19, 18, ...

Challenge 3 Trace the line and count on.

21, 22, 23, ...

Number

Lesson 2: **Reading numbers to 20**

• Read numbers from 0 to 20

Challenge 1 Count and draw a line to the right number.

1	2	3	4	5	6	7	8	9	10

Challenge 2 Count and draw a line to the right number.

1	2	3	4	5	6	7	8	9	10
11	12	13	14	15	16	17	18	19	20

Challenge 3 Draw flowers to match the numbers.

7	14

Lesson 3: **Writing numbers to 20**

• Write numbers from 0 to 20

Challenge 1 Trace over the numbers.

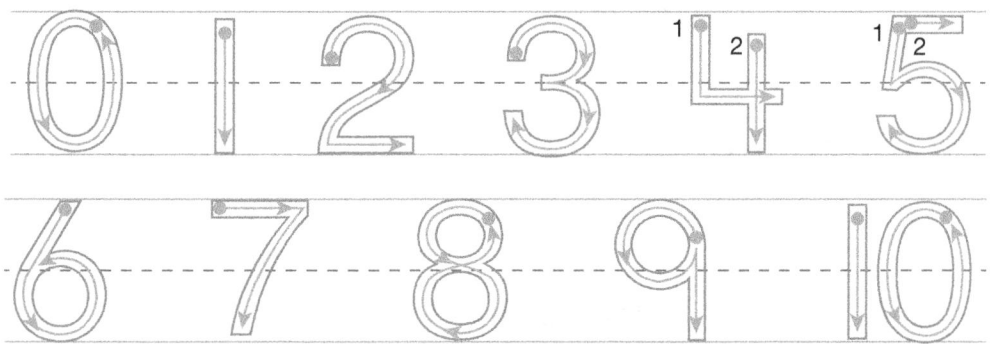

Challenge 2 Trace over the numbers.

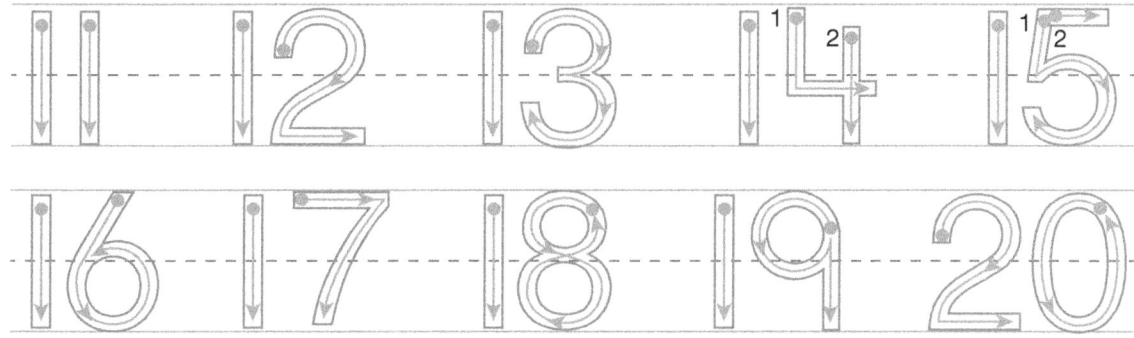

Challenge 3 Fill in the missing numbers.

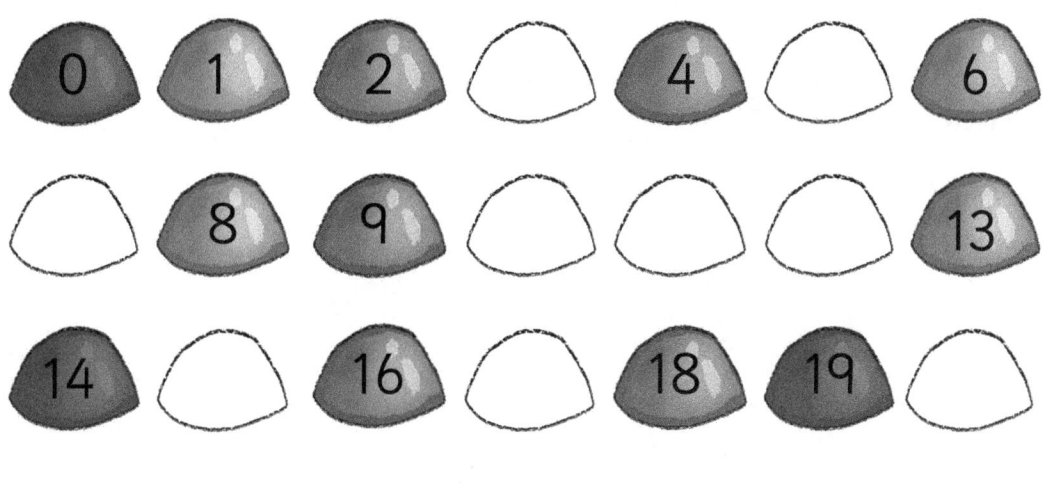

Number

Lesson 4: **Counting objects**

• Count up to 20 objects

You will need
• pile of counters

Challenge 1

Count the circles.
Tick each one as you count it.

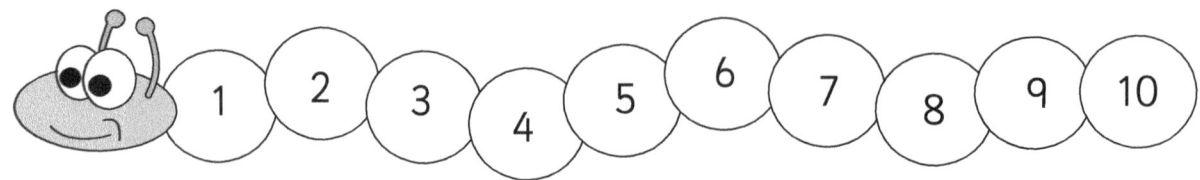

Challenge 2

Count out 7 counters. Draw around each one.

How many counters have you drawn?

Challenge 3

Circle each flower as you count it.
How many are there?

Number

Lesson 5: **Counting in 2s (1)**

• Count in 2s

 Challenge 1 Trace the line to count in 2s.

0   1   2   3   4   5   6   7   8   9   10

Challenge 2 Count in 2s.

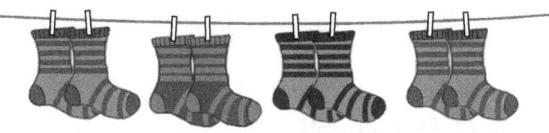

1 How many socks are there?

2 How many shoes are there?

3 How many gloves are there?

Challenge 3 Draw 5 pairs of socks. How many are there altogether? Count in 2s.

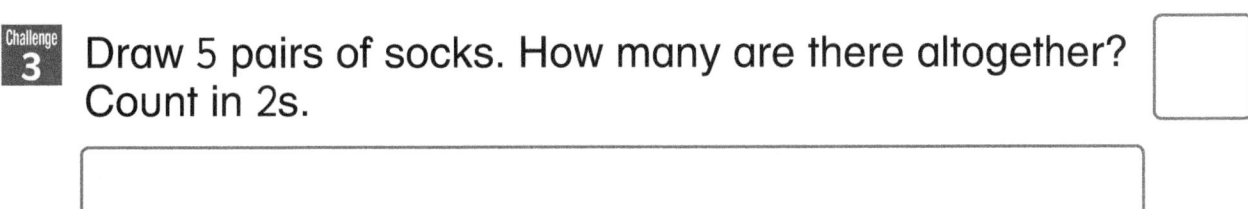

Lesson 6: **Counting in 10s (1)**

• Count in 10s

Number

Challenge 1 Count on in 10s.

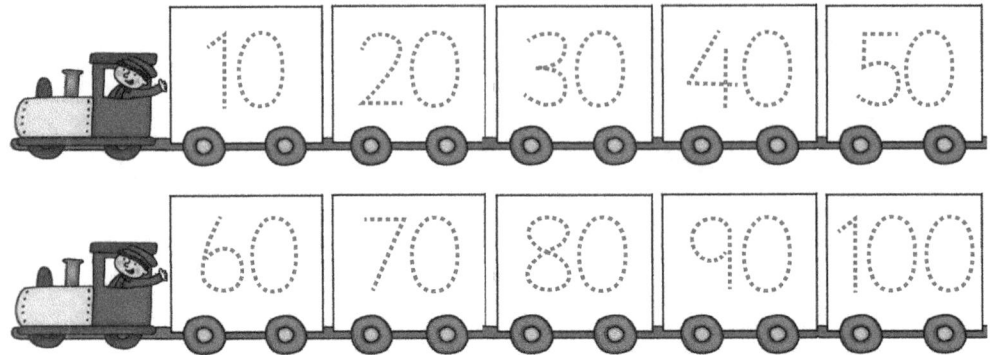

Challenge 2 Count on in 10s. Fill in the missing numbers.

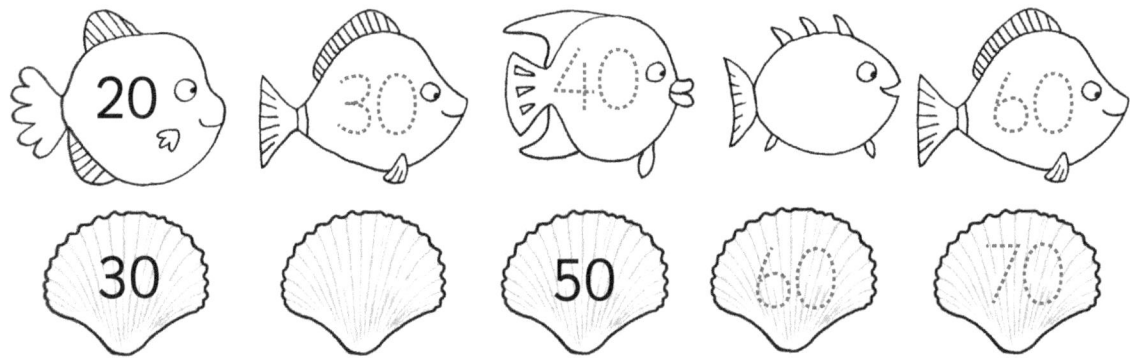

Challenge 3 Count on in 10s and fill in the missing numbers.

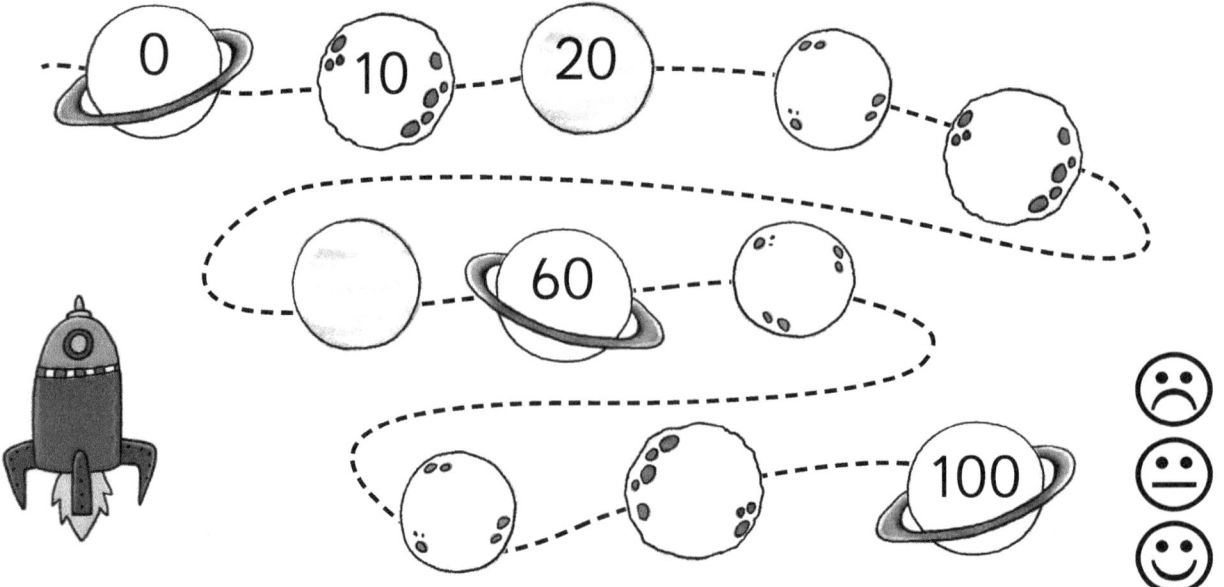

Lesson 7: **Ordering numbers**

- Order numbers to at least 20

1	2	3	4	5	6	7	8	9	10	11	12	13	14	15	16	17	18	19	20

Number

Challenge 1 Order the numbers from smallest to largest.

8 2 5

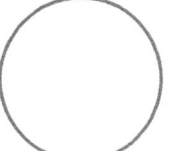

6 2 1

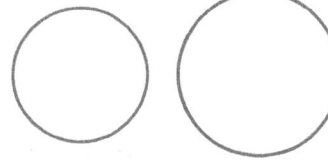

Challenge 2 Order the numbers from smallest to largest.

16 14 9

20 8 17

Challenge 3 Order the numbers from largest to smallest.

21 25 11

17 14 18

9

Lesson 8: **Estimating**

- Estimate how many objects there are and check this by counting

Challenge 1 Estimate, then count.

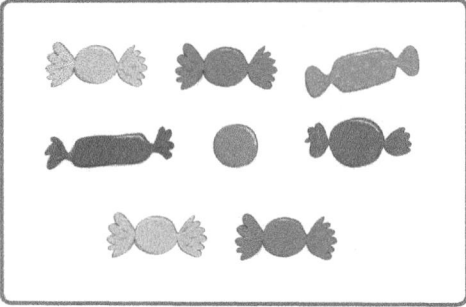

Estimate

Count

Challenge 2 Estimate, then count.

Estimate

Count

Estimate

Count

Challenge 3 Estimate, then count.

Estimate

Count

• Count on in 2s

Number

Challenge 1 Count in 2s.

Challenge 2 **1** Count on in 2s.

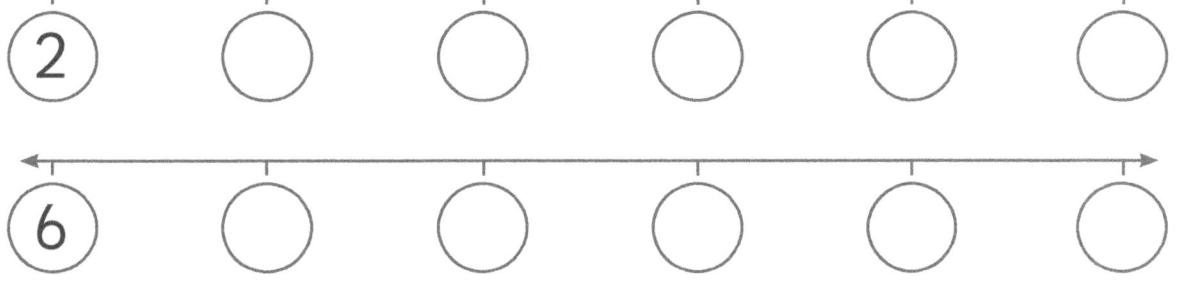

(2) ( ) ( ) ( ) ( ) ( )

(6) ( ) ( ) ( ) ( ) ( )

2 Fill in the missing numbers.

2 4 6   10   16   20

1 3   7   13 15   19

Challenge 3 Start at the circled numbers. Count on 5 sets of 2.
Colour the numbers you finish on.

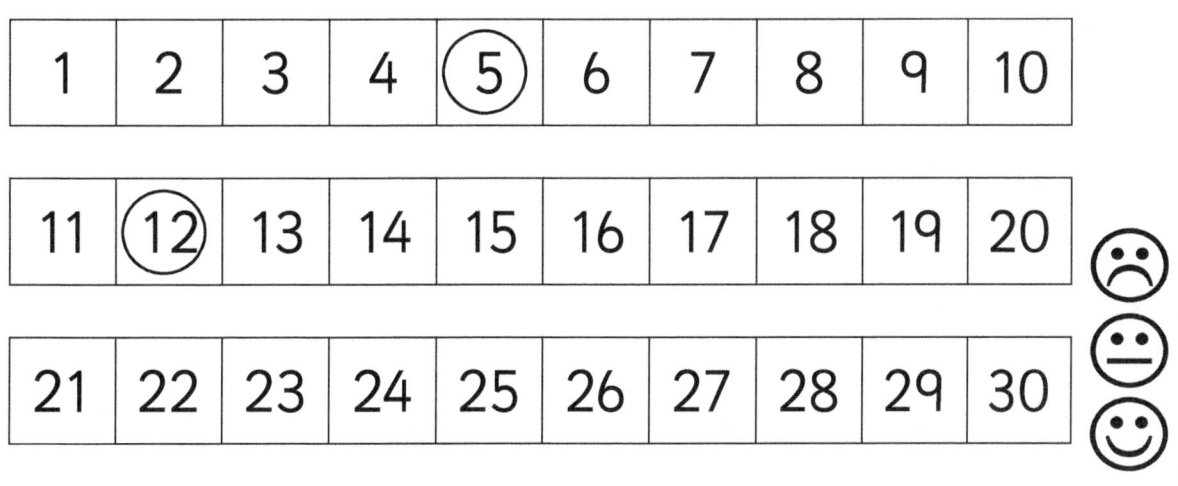

| 1 | 2 | 3 | 4 | (5) | 6 | 7 | 8 | 9 | 10 |

| 11 | (12) | 13 | 14 | 15 | 16 | 17 | 18 | 19 | 20 |

| 21 | 22 | 23 | 24 | 25 | 26 | 27 | 28 | 29 | 30 |

• Recognise odd and even numbers

Number

Challenge 1 How many flowers? [ ] Odd or even? [ ]

Challenge 2 **1** How many leaves? [ ] Odd or even? [ ]

2 Write odd numbers. [ ] [ ] [ ] [ ] [ ]

3 Write even numbers. [ ] [ ] [ ] [ ] [ ]

Challenge 3 Circle the odd numbers.

7, 12, 54, 3, 15, 78, 60, 21, 33, 26

Lesson 3: **Counting in 10s (2)**

- Count in 10s

You will need
- 100 square

 Challenge 1 Count on in 10s.

10   30

60   80

 Challenge 2 **1** Start at 4. Count on in 10s.

4   24   44

74   94

2 Start at 6. Count on in 10s.

6

56

Challenge 3 Start at 3. Count on in 10s.

• Say the number that is 1 or 10 more or less

You will need
• 100 square

Challenge 1

Find 1 less and 1 more than each number.

1 ☐ ⟨ 1 less | **8** | 1 more ⟩ ☐

2 ☐ ⟨ 1 less | **17** | 1 more ⟩ ☐

3 ☐ ⟨ 1 less | **25** | 1 more ⟩ ☐

Challenge 2

1 Find 1 more and 10 more.

a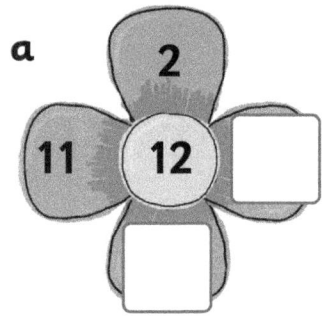

b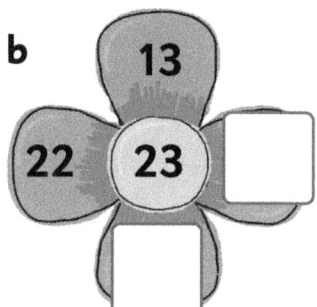

2 Find 1 less and 10 less.

a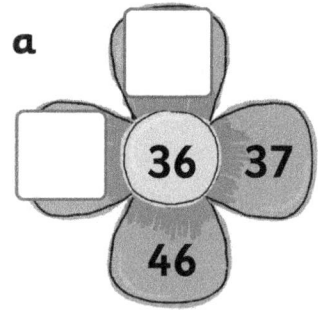

b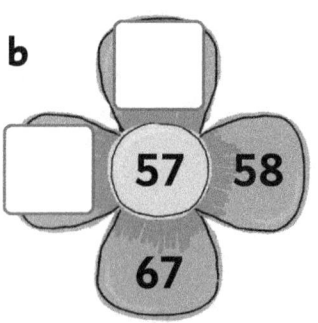

Challenge 3

Find 1 more and less and 10 more and less.

1  28

2 75

3 89

Lesson 5: **Comparing and ordering numbers**

- Compare and order numbers
- Give a number between two numbers

 Challenge 1 Fill in using the numbers in the box. You can use the numbers more than once.

| 3 | 6 | 7 | 9 | 12 | 15 | 17 |

1 [ ] ⟨less than⟩ ☆ 6 ⟨more than⟩ [ ]

2 [ ] ⟨less than⟩ ☆ 15 ⟨more than⟩ [ ]

3 [ ] ⟨less than⟩ ☆ 9 ⟨more than⟩ [ ]

 Challenge 2 Complete the number track with numbers from the box.

| 14 | 2 | 12 | 7 | 17 |
| 4 | 18 | 9 | 15 | 6 |

| 1 | | 3 | | 5 | |

| 13 | | 11 | 10 | | 8 |

| | 16 | | | 19 | 20 |

Challenge 3 Fill in the boxes so that the numbers are in order.

1 2 [ ] 5 [ ] 8

2 8 [ ] 10 [ ] 13

3 6 [ ] [ ] 22 [ ] [ ] 33

4 19 [ ] [ ] 28 [ ] [ ] 40

15

Lesson 6: **Ordinal numbers**

• Use ordinal numbers to show position

Challenge 1 Write the ordinal numbers on the carriages in order.

| 1st | 2nd | | 4th | | | 7th | 8th | | 10th |

Challenge 2 Write the ordinal numbers on the crocodiles in order.

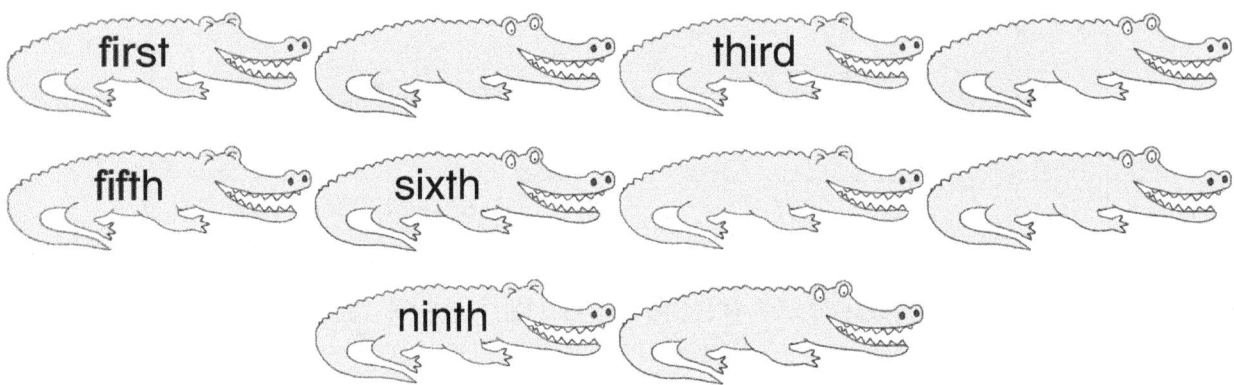

first   third

fifth   sixth

ninth

Challenge 3 **1** Label the carriages.

1st

2 Which position is the …

16

• Partition 2-digit numbers into tens and ones

Challenge 1 Find the missing 10 or 1.

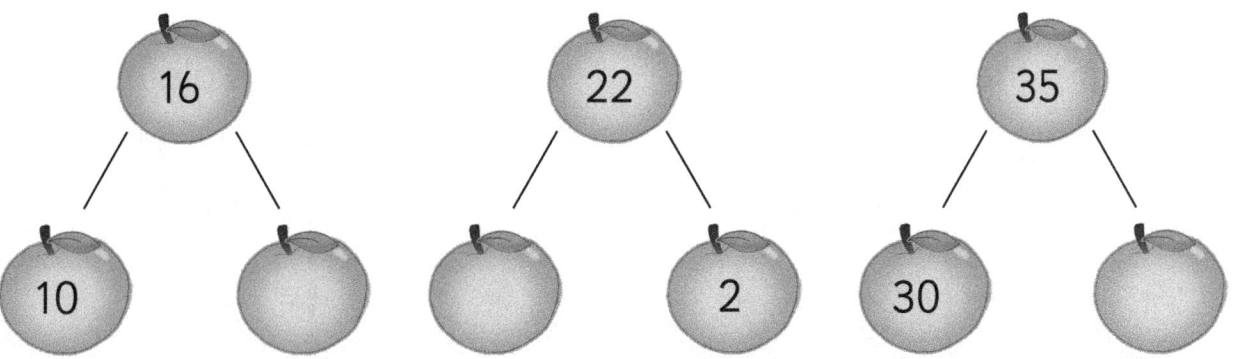

16 / 10 / ___

22 / ___ / 2

35 / 30 / ___

Challenge 2 Write the number shown.

1 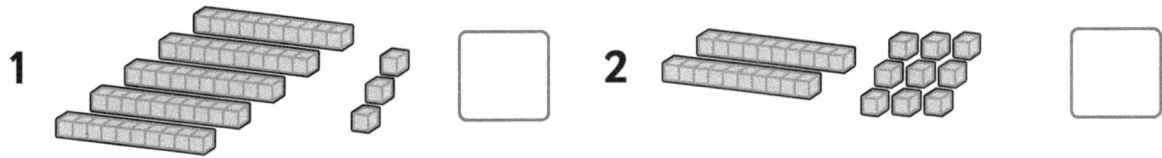 ☐

2 ☐

3 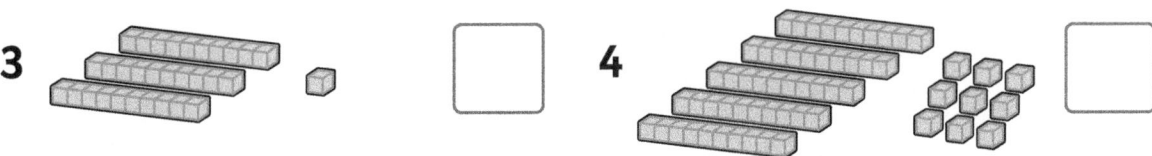 ☐

4 ☐

Challenge 3 Write the number shown.

1  ☐

2 ☐

3 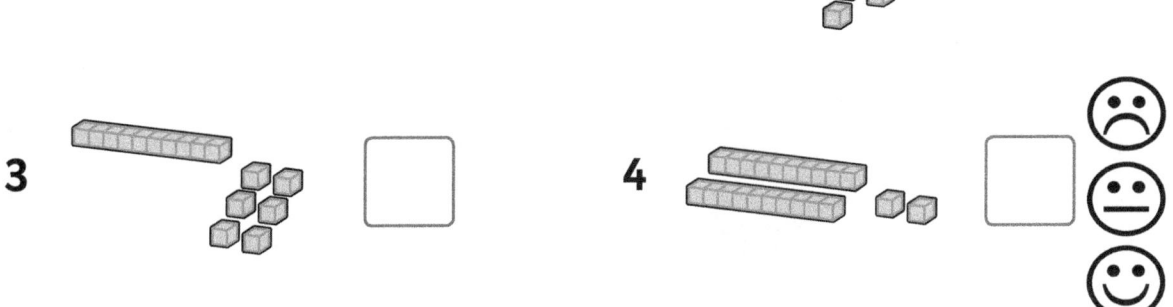 ☐

4 ☐

☹
😐
🙂

Number

• Partition 2-digit numbers into tens and ones
• Write a 2-digit number written as tens and ones

You will need
• coloured pencils

Challenge 1 Colour the ones digit.

Colour the tens digit.

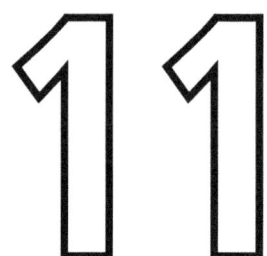

Challenge 2 Fill in the tens and ones.

1

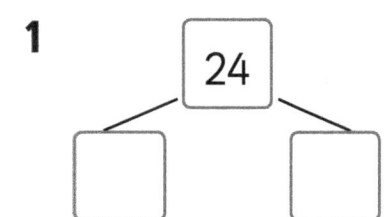
24

2

67

3

35

4

43

Challenge 3 Partition the numbers and write the numbers in the boxes.

1

16

2

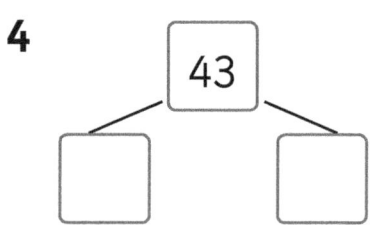
92

☐ + ☐ = 16

☐ + ☐ = 92

18

Number

• Say the number that is 1 or 10 more or less

 Match the numbers that are 1 more and 1 less.

17   22   31   23   32

30   15   24   16   24

 1 Find 1 more and 1 less than and 10 more and 10 less.

a 18   **b** 13   **c** 10

2 Find the missing number.

a

8
17   19
28

b

1
10   12
21

c
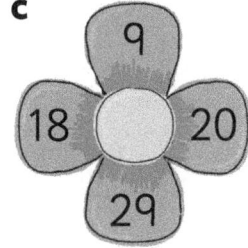
9
18   20
29

 Find the missing numbers.

1 22

2 30

3 14

19

Number

• Compare two numbers
• Give a number that lies in between two numbers

Challenge 1

1 Circle the larger number.

15 17   4 2   10 11   20 12

2 Circle the smaller number.

3 7   18 19   16 14   8 11

Challenge 2

1 Circle the larger number.

76 32   24 42   80 60   21 12

2 Circle the smaller number.

53 35   18 81   74 61   95 25

3 Complete the number lines.

a 51 ☐ ☐ ☐ 55

b 7 ☐☐☐☐☐☐☐☐☐☐☐☐ 20

c 39 ☐ 41

Challenge 3

Make these sentences true.

1 ☐4☐ is larger than ☐ .

2 ☐ is smaller than ☐12☐ .

3 ☐15☐ is larger than ☐ but smaller than ☐ .

Lesson 3: **Tens and ones**

• Find the tens and ones digits of a 2-digit number

Number

Challenge 1 Find the tens and ones.

1

48

tens ones

☐ ☐

2

26

tens ones

☐ ☐

3

75

tens ones

☐ ☐

Challenge 2 Match each number to the place value cards.

1 | 6 | 0 |▷

2 | 2 | 0 |▷

3 | 1 | 0 |▷

4 | 3 | 0 |▷

5 | 4 | 0 |▷

☆ 33

☆ 61

☆ 29

☆ 47

☆ 15

| 7 |▷

| 3 |▷

| 1 |▷

| 9 |▷

| 5 |▷

Challenge 3 Fill in the tens and ones and write the number sentence.

1

48

tens ones

☐ ☐

☐ + ☐ = ☐

2

26

tens ones

☐ ☐

☐ + ☐ = ☐

3

75

tens ones

☐ ☐

☐ + ☐ = ☐

Lesson 4: **Splitting numbers**

• Find the tens and ones digits of a 2-digit number

Number

Challenge 1 Write the number, find the tens and ones.

	Number	Tens	Ones

Challenge 2 Match the picture to the number. Then split into tens and ones.

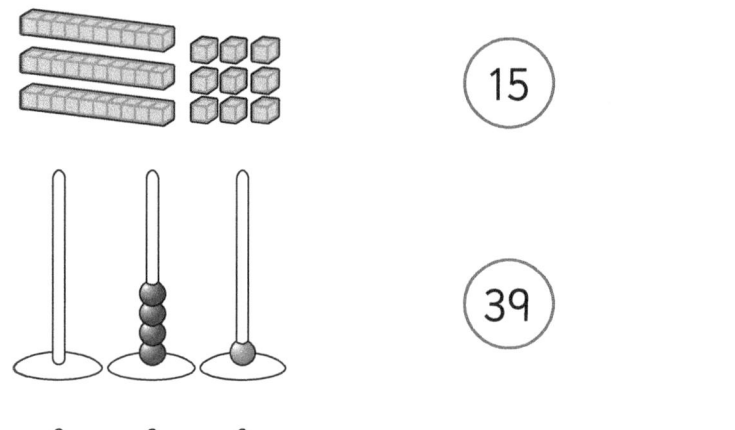

15

tens ones

39

tens ones

41

tens ones

Challenge 3 Draw and write to complete the table.

	Number	Tens	Ones
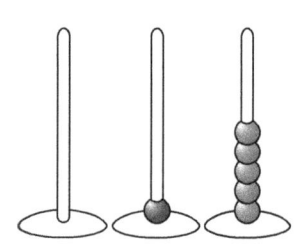			
		5	7

22

Lesson 1: **Halves of objects**

- Find half of an object
- Recognise objects that are in halves

 Draw lines to match the halves.

 Circle the food that is in halves.

Draw lines to halve the chocolate bars.

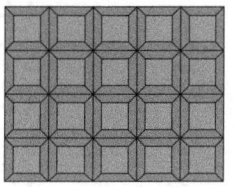 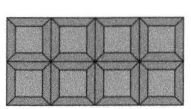 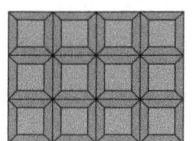 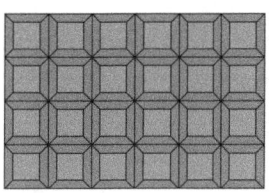

Lesson 2: **Halves of shapes**

Number

- Find half of a shape
- Recognise a shape that is in halves

Challenge 1 Tick the shapes that are cut in half.

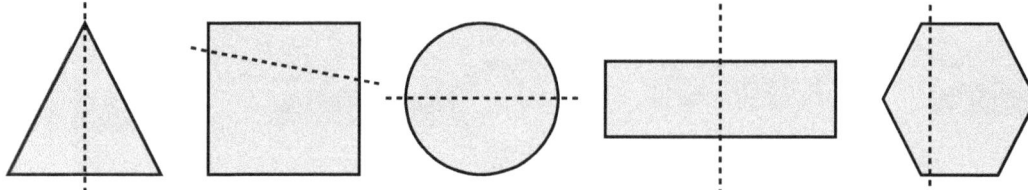

Challenge 2   **1** Match each shape to its half.

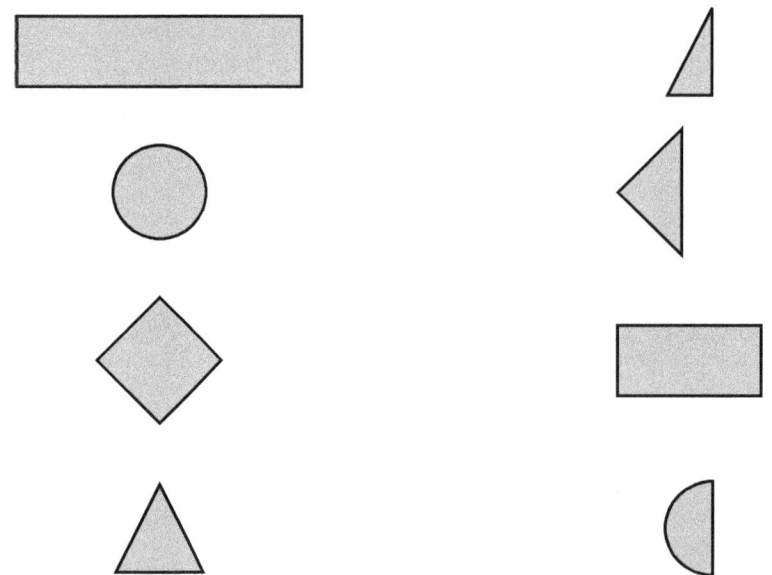

2 Draw a line to cut each shape in half.

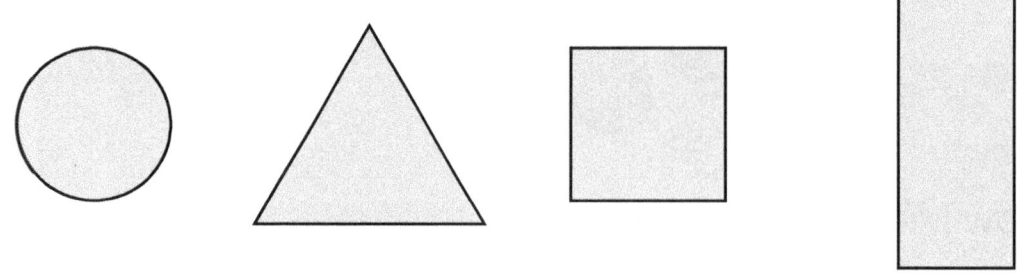

Challenge 3 Show four ways you can cut a square in half.

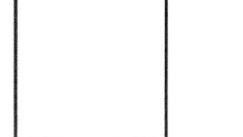   

24

Lesson 3: **Halves of amounts (1)**

• Find half of an amount

 **Challenge 1** Circle the groups that have been halved.

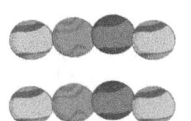    

 Challenge 2 Share the toys equally. How many do they get each?

1

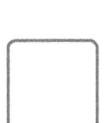

2

3

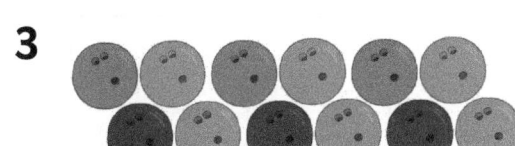

4

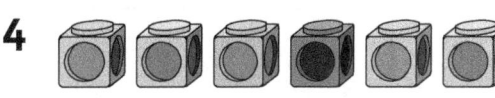

 Challenge 3 Find half of each group.

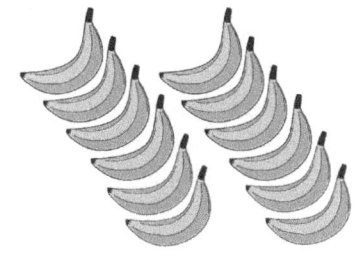

Lesson 4: **Halves of amounts (2)**

Unit **4**

Number

• Find half of an amount

Challenge 1
Can you share the cakes equally?
Draw dots to make the halves equal.

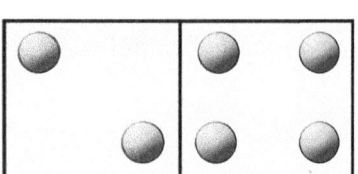
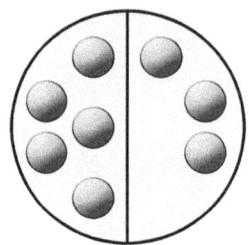
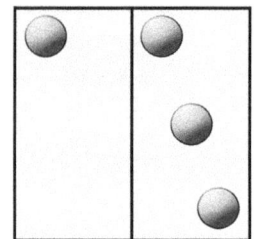
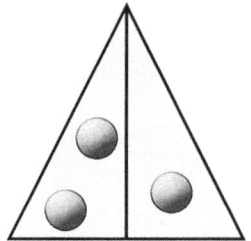

Challenge 2
Divide each group in half.

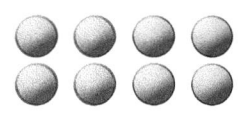
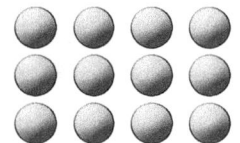

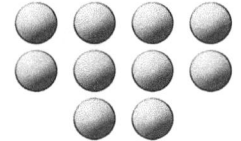

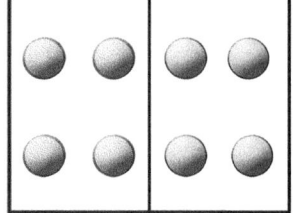
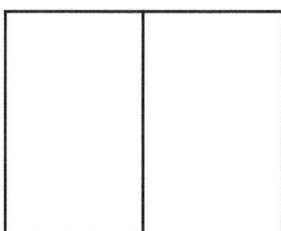
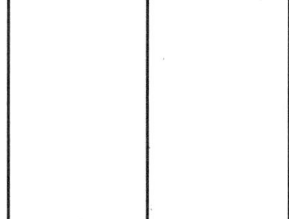
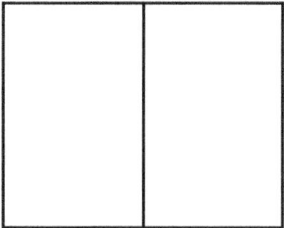

Challenge 3
Share the cakes equally. How many will each child get?

Number

• Find half of a number

 Challenge 1   Draw dots to find half.

1
8

2
6

3
12

4
14

5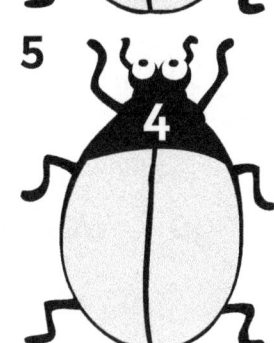
4

6
20

Challenge 2   1   Find half.

a | Half of 10 | ➡ | |

b | Half of 16 | ➡ | |

c | Half of 28 | ➡ | |

d | Half of 24 | ➡ | |

2   Draw dots to show half.

30 | | |

Challenge 3   Find the number before it was halved.

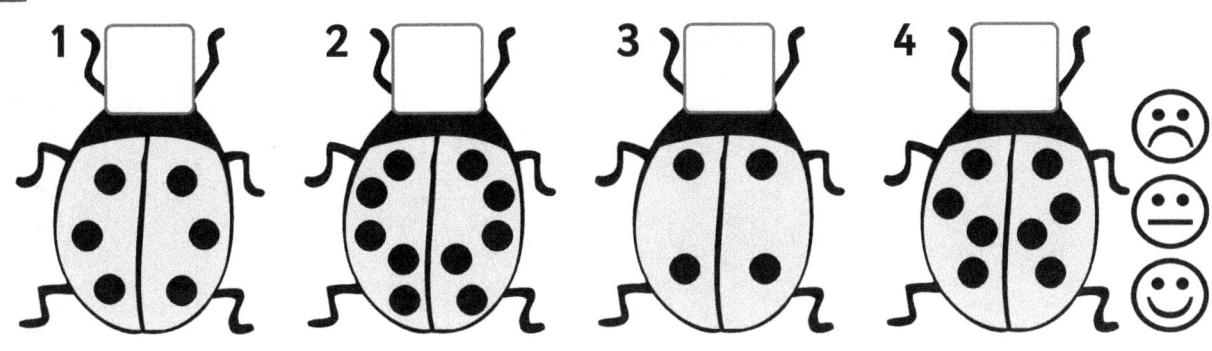

27

Lesson 6: **Halves of numbers (2)**

Number

• Find half of a number

Challenge 1

Use the strings to work out half.

1 (20) 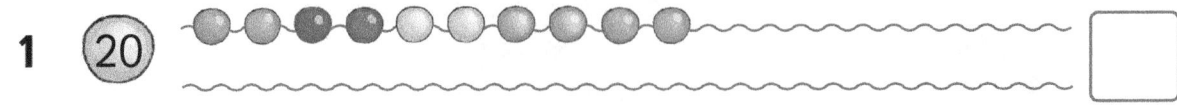 ☐

2 (14)  ☐

3 (18) 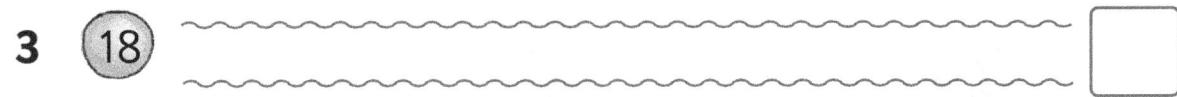 ☐

Challenge 2

Draw beads on the strings to work out half.

1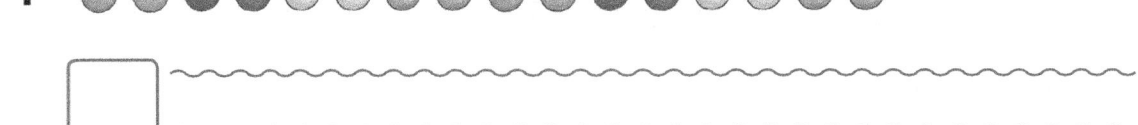

☐

2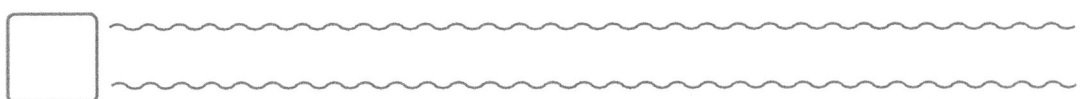

☐

3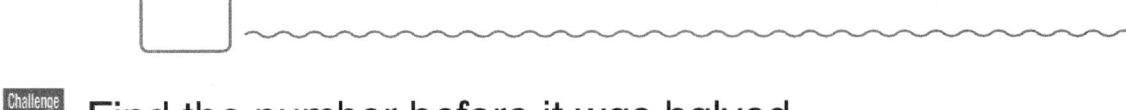

☐

Challenge 3

Find the number before it was halved.

1 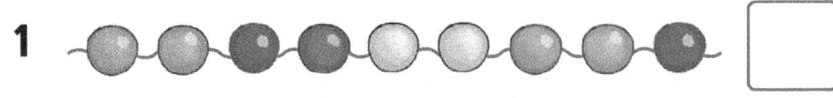 ☐

2 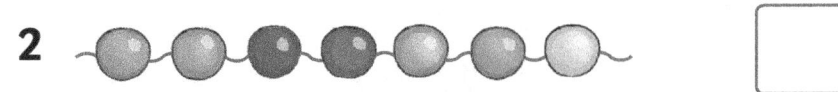 ☐

Lesson 7: **Halves in measures**

• Find halves when measuring

You will need
• coloured pencils

Challenge 1

Circle the cups that are half full.

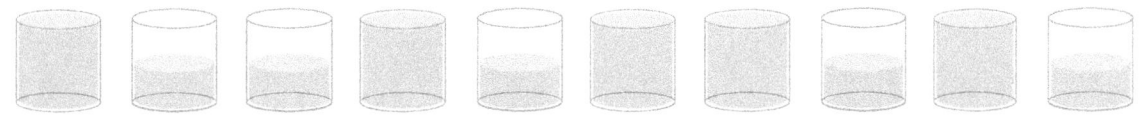

Challenge 2

1 Find half the length in cubes.

a [ ] cubes **b** [ ] cubes

2 Colour the cubes to show half.

a

b

c

d

Challenge 3

Make the scales balance.

1 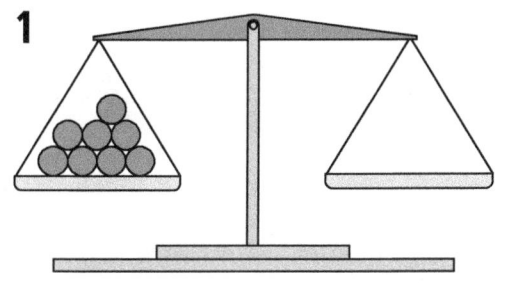 **2**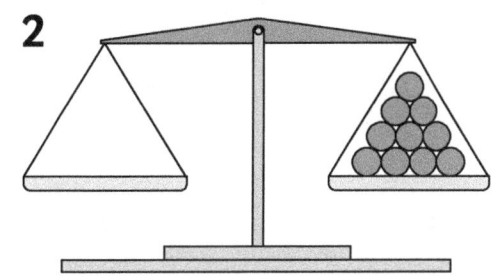

29

Lesson 8: **Combining halves**

Number

• Put 2 halves together to make a whole

Challenge 1 Count the halves.

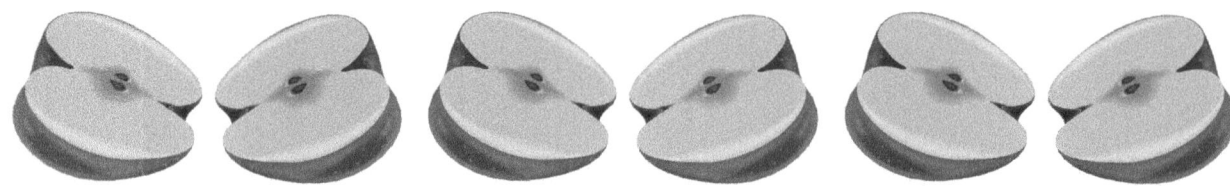

There are ☐ whole apples.

Challenge 2

1 Count the halves.

    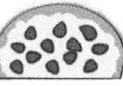   

There are ☐ whole cakes.

2 Count the halves.

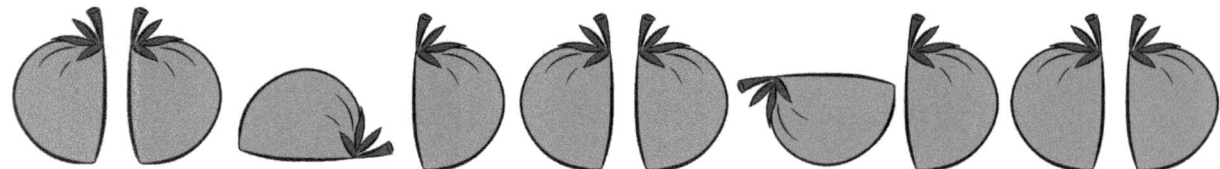

There are ☐ whole tomatoes.

Challenge 3 Count the halves.

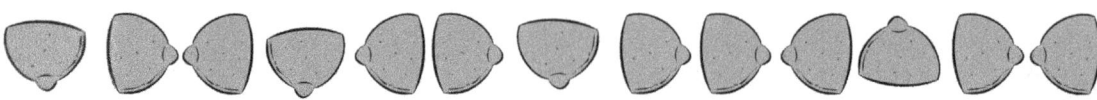

There are ☐ whole lemons.

• Combine two sets of objects by counting them all

Challenge 1 Count each set. Then count how many altogether.

1

☐ + ☐ = ☐

2

☐ + ☐ = ☐

Challenge 2 Count how many altogether.

1  + ... = ☐

2  + ... = ☐

3  = ☐

4  = ☐

Challenge 3 Match each set to the right total.

5

7

12

3

14

31

Lesson 2: **Addition: counting on**

Number

• Add two numbers together by counting on

Challenge 1 Add by counting on.

1 4 and 2 = ☐

2 5 and 4 = ☐

Challenge 2 Add by counting on. Start from the larger number.

1 7 and 1 ☐

2 2 and 6 ☐

3 3 and 9 ☐

4 11 and 4 ☐

Challenge 3 Use the number line to add. Count on from the larger number.

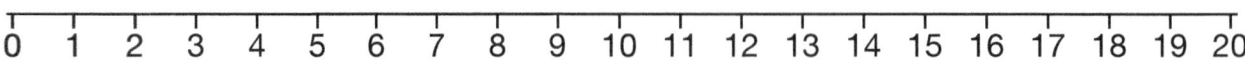

1 13 and 7 ☐

2 5 and 12 ☐

3 4 and 15 ☐

4 8 and 9 ☐

Lesson 3: **Addition**: number bonds for 10

- Identify pairs of numbers that make 10

You will need
- coloured pencils

Challenge 1 Colour enough cubes to make 10.

1

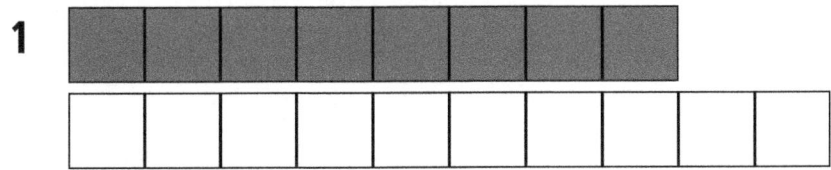

2

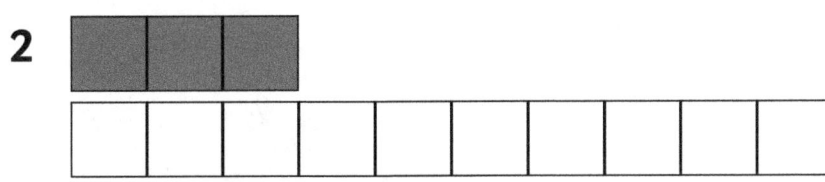

3

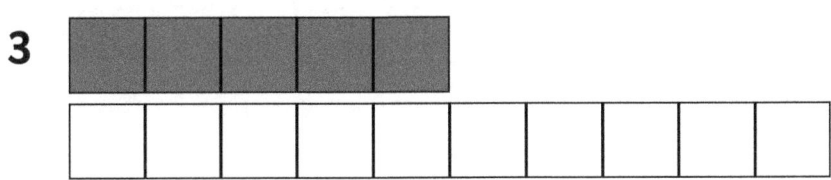

Challenge 2 Match the eggs to make 10.

1   2   3   4   5

5   6   7   8   9

Challenge 3 Write as many ways as you can to make 10.

☐ + ☐ = 10   ☐ + ☐ = 10   ☐ + ☐ = 10

☐ + ☐ = 10   ☐ + ☐ = 10   ☐ + ☐ = 10

☐ + ☐ = 10   ☐ + ☐ = 10

☐ + ☐ = 10   ☐ + ☐ = 10

• Find pairs of numbers that add up to numbers from 2 to 10

Challenge 1 Draw more beads to make the right amount.

1 4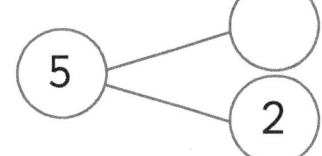

2 8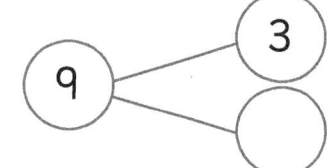

3 6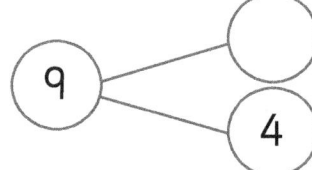

Challenge 2 Complete the number bonds.

1

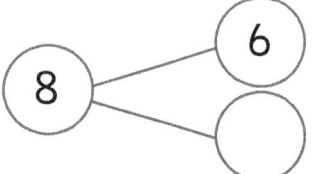

2

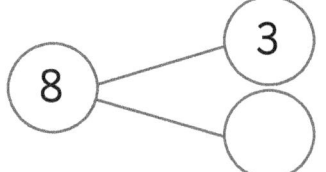

3

Challenge 3 Circle the incorrect number bond.

1

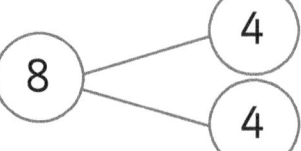

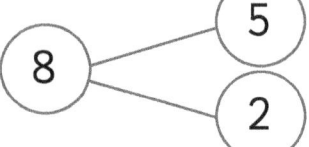

2

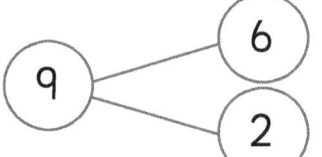

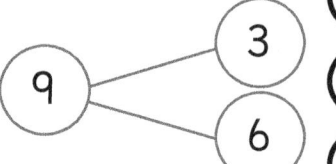

Lesson 5: **Subtraction**: taking away

• Subtract a number by taking away objects

 Take away. How many are left?

1 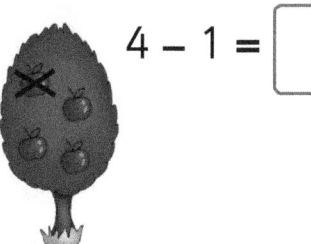 4 − 1 = ☐   **2** 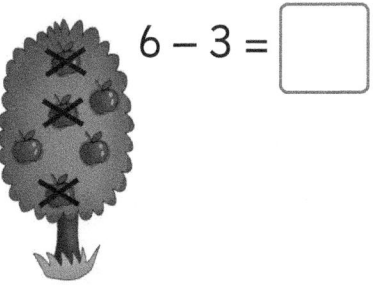 6 − 3 = ☐

 1 Take away the number shown. How many are left?

a  = ☐

b  = ☐

2 Show the sum by crossing out the buttons.
Then write the answer.

a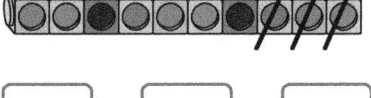

6 − 2 = ☐

b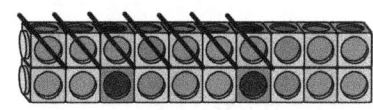

10 − 4 = ☐

 Write the subtraction and complete the answer.

1

☐ − ☐ = ☐

2

☐ − ☐ = ☐

35

Number

• Subtract one number from another by counting back

Challenge 1 Take away these numbers from 5.

1 2 ☐ **2** 4 ☐ **3** 1 ☐

Challenge 2 Take away by counting back.

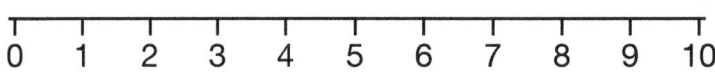

1 10 − 7 = ☐ **2** 8 − 4 = ☐ **3** 6 − 1 = ☐

Challenge 3 Subtract by finding the larger number and counting back.

1 Ayesha had 9 marbles, but she dropped 3.

How many does she have now?

2 Sam had 10 sweets but gave 2 to his dad.

How many does he have left?

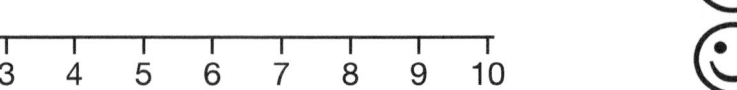

Lesson 7: **Subtraction: finding the difference**

• Find the difference between two numbers

Challenge 1 Find the difference between the shaded numbers.

1  **3**

2  ☐

Challenge 2 Use the number line to find the difference.

1 7 and 10 ☐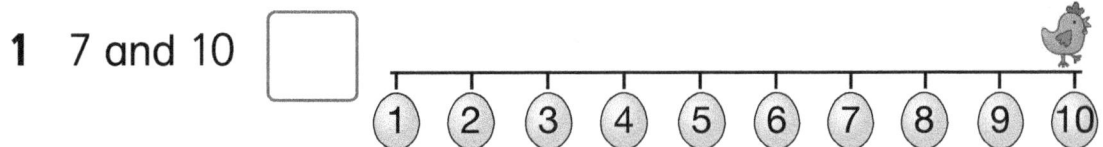

2 1 and 7 ☐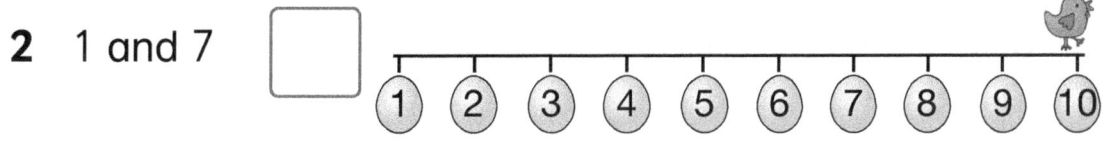

3 3 and 9 ☐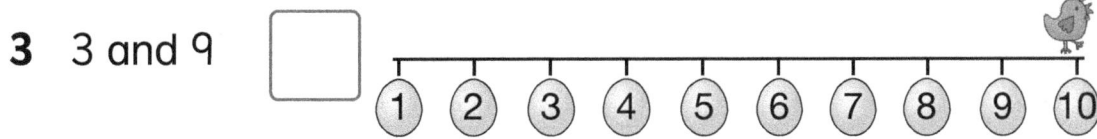

Challenge 3 Use the number line to find the difference.

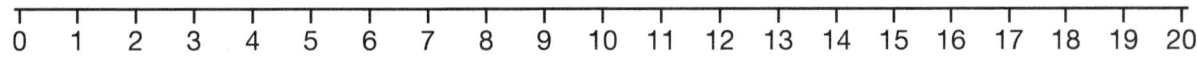

1 🐟 9 and 🐟 17 ☐   **2** ⭐ 6 and ⭐ 14 ☐

3 🍎 4 and 🍎 20 ☐   **4** 🍬 7 and 🍬 12 = ☐

37

Number

• Use number bonds for 10 to answer subtraction calculations

Challenge 1 Complete the subtractions.

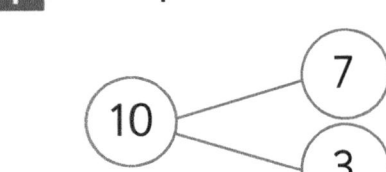 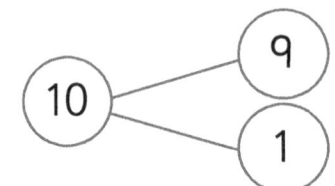 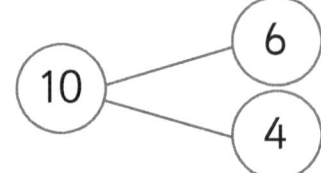

1 $10 - 7 = \boxed{}$ **2** $10 - 1 = \boxed{}$ **3** $10 - 4 = \boxed{}$

Challenge 2 **1** Complete the bond and write the subtraction.

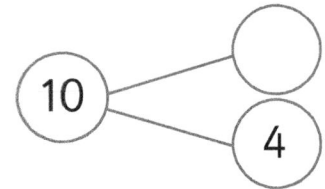 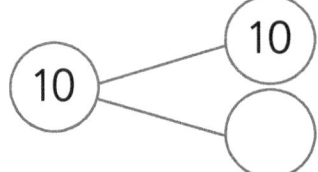 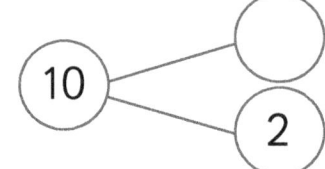

a $10 - \boxed{} = \boxed{}$ **b** $10 - \boxed{} = \boxed{}$ **c** $10 - \boxed{} = \boxed{}$

2 Complete the bond to match the subtraction.

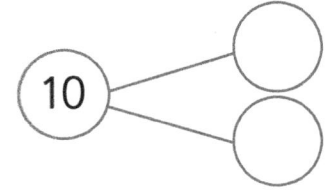 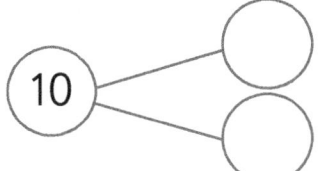 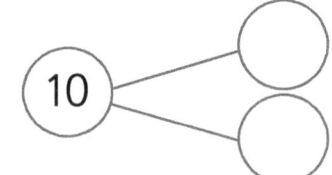

a $10 - 9 = 1$ **b** $10 - 5 = 5$ **c** $10 - 6 = 4$

Challenge 3 Make your own bonds and write subtractions to match.

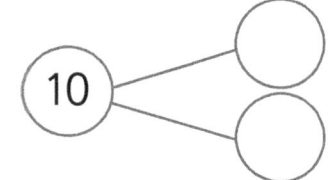 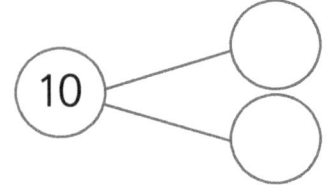

1 $10 - \boxed{} = \boxed{}$ **2** $10 - \boxed{} = \boxed{}$

Lesson 1: **Recording calculations**

- Write number sentences for addition and subtraction calculations

Challenge 1 Complete the number sentences.

1 Add:

| 4 | + | 3 | = | |

2 Take away:

| 7 | − | | ◯ | 5 |

Challenge 2 Write a number sentence to match each picture.

1 Add:

▢ ◯ ▢ ◯ ▢

2 Add:

▢ ◯ ▢ ◯ ▢

3 Take away:

▢ ◯ ▢ ◯ ▢

4 Take away:

▢ ◯ ▢ ◯ ▢

Challenge 3 Write a number sentence for the problem.

A pet shop has 7 fish. 2 are bought. How many are left?

▢ ◯ ▢ ◯ ▢

Lesson 2: **Adding two single-digit numbers (1)**

• Add single-digit numbers together

Challenge 1

Use a number line to add these numbers.

1 4 + 3 = 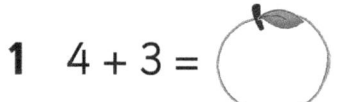   **2** 6 + 2 = 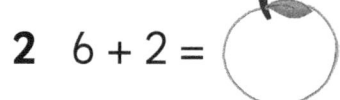   **3** 5 + 5 =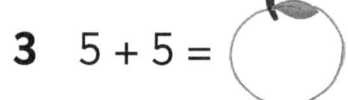

Challenge 2

1 Use a number line to add these numbers.

a 7 + 4 = 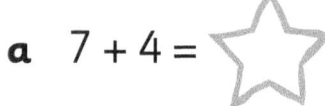   **b** 9 + 5 = 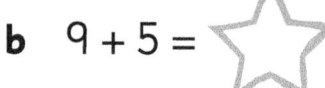   **c** 4 + 8 =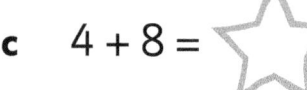

2 Write number sentences to match these problems.

a Tom makes a tower of 6 bricks. He adds 1 more. How many are there altogether?

b Rachel puts 7 strawberries on a plate then asks for 2 more. How many are there altogether?

Challenge 3

Write number sentences to match these problems.

1 Will has 9 toy cars. He is given 8 more. How many does he have now?

2 Olivia picks 7 oranges. Lucy picks 6. How many do they have altogether?

• Check answers to additions and subtractions

Challenge 1 Are these number sentences correct? Complete the checking number sentences to find out. Put a ✓ if they are right and a ✗ if they are wrong.

1 | 5 + 2 = 7 | 2 + 5 = [7] | ✓   **2** | 5 − 2 = 6 | 6 + 2 = [ ] | [ ]

3 | 4 + 5 = 8 | 5 + 4 = [ ] | [ ]   **4** | 4 − 1 = 3 | 3 + 1 = [ ] | [ ]

Challenge 2 **1** Add the numbers in a different order to check.

a 6 + 3 = 9   **b** 7 + 2 = 8   **c** 4 + 3 = 10

[ ] + [ ] = [ ]   [ ] + [ ] = [ ]   [ ] + [ ] = [ ]

2 Check the subtractions by adding the answer and the smaller number together.

a 10 − 6 = 2   **b** 5 − 4 = 1   **c** 9 − 3 = 2

[ ] + [ ] = [ ]   [ ] + [ ] = [ ]   [ ] + [ ] = [ ]

Challenge 3 Write a number sentence to check the answers.

1 15 − 5 = 10 [ ]   **2** 12 + 4 = 17 [ ]

3 13 − 9 = 3 [ ]   **4** 14 + 2 = 16 [ ]

Number

41

Lesson 4: **Addition and subtraction number bonds for 10 (1)**

- Know addition and subtraction number bonds for 10

Number

Challenge 1 Fill in the missing numbers.

1 $10 - 1 = \boxed{}$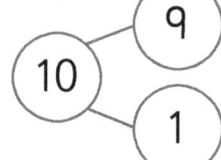

2 $10 - \boxed{} = 8$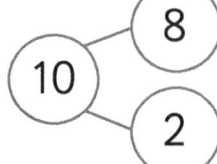

3 $3 + \boxed{} = 10$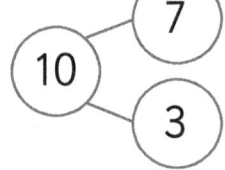

4 $5 + 5 = \boxed{}$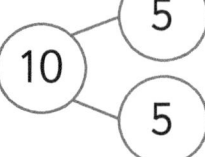

Challenge 2 Fill in the missing numbers.

1 $6 + \boxed{} = \boxed{}$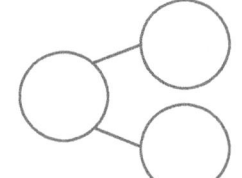

2 $10 - \boxed{} = \boxed{}$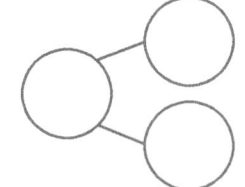

3 $10 - \boxed{} = 9$

4 $\boxed{} + 2 = 10$

Challenge 3 Make your own number bonds and write sentences.

1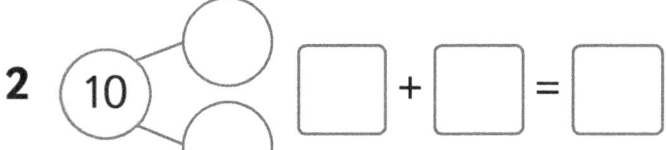

2

42

• Use number bonds for 10 to make 10, then add more

Challenge 1 First make 10, then add what's left over.

1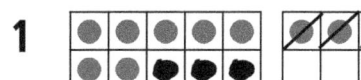

2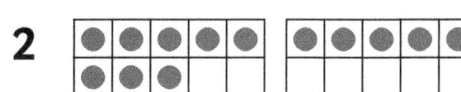

Challenge 2 First make 10, then add what's left over.

1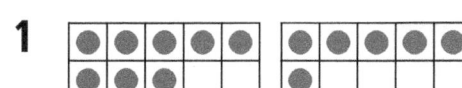

☐ + ☐ = ☐

2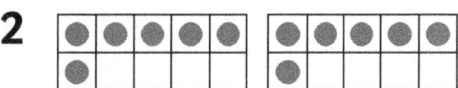

☐ + ☐ = ☐

3

☐ + ☐ = ☐

4

☐ + ☐ = ☐

Challenge 3 Complete the additions, making 10 first.

1 5 + 7

$$5 + 5 + 2 = 12$$

2 7 + 7

☐ + ☐ + ☐ = ☐

3 6 + 5

☐ + ☐ + ☐ = ☐

4 8 + 7

☐ + ☐ + ☐ = ☐

43

Lesson 6: **Adding more than two numbers**

• Add more than two numbers, finding number bonds for 10 to help you

You will need
• coloured pencils

Number

Challenge 1 Colour the groups that make 10, then count on to find the answer.

1 $9 + 1 + 3 = \boxed{}$

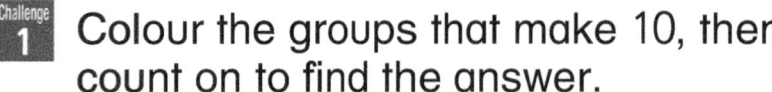

2 $8 + 4 + 2 = \boxed{}$

Challenge 2 Circle the numbers that make 10, then complete the number sentence.

1 $\boxed{8} + \boxed{2} + \boxed{3}$

$10 + \boxed{} = \boxed{}$

2 $1 + 9 + 2$

$10 + \boxed{} = \boxed{}$

3 $3 + 4 + 7$

$10 + \boxed{} = \boxed{}$

4 $5 + 5 + 1$

$10 + \boxed{} = \boxed{}$

Challenge 3 Write 3-number additions to make 14, first using bonds to 10.

$\boxed{} + \boxed{} + \boxed{} = 14$ $\boxed{} + \boxed{} + \boxed{} = 14$

$\boxed{} + \boxed{} + \boxed{} = 14$ $\boxed{} + \boxed{} + \boxed{} = 14$

Lesson 7: **2 more or less**

• Use a number line to find 2 more or less

Challenge 1 Jump the frog forwards to find 2 more.

1

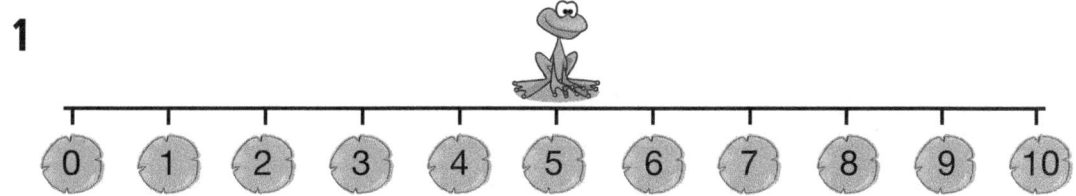

2

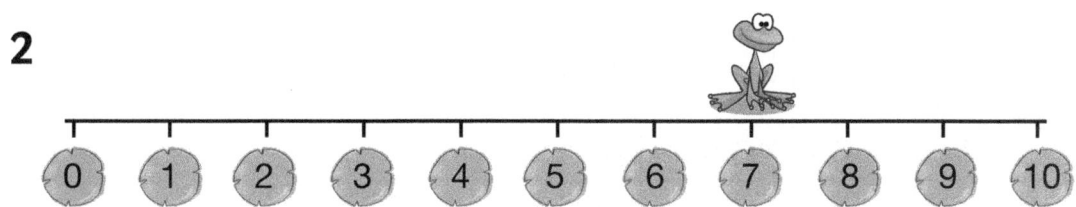

Challenge 2 Circle the numbers that are 2 more and 2 less than the starting number. Show your jumps on the number line.

1 0 1 2 3 4 5 6 7 8 9 10 11 (12) 13 14 15 16 17 18 19 20

2 0 1 2 3 4 5 6 7 8 9 10 11 12 13 14 15 16 17 (18) 19 20

3 0 1 2 3 (4) 5 6 7 8 9 10 11 12 13 14 15 16 17 18 19 20

Challenge 3 Write the numbers that are 2 more and 2 less than the starting number. Show your jumps on the number line.

1

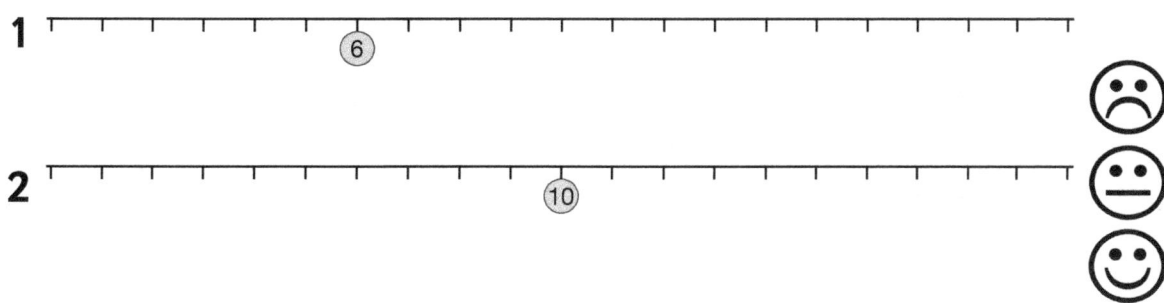

6

2

10

45

Lesson 8: **10 more or less**

Number

• Find 10 more or less

You will need
• coloured pencils

1	2	3	4	5	6	7	8	9	10
11	12	13	14	15	16	17	18	19	20
21	22	23	24	25	26	27	28	29	30
31	32	33	34	35	36	37	38	39	40
41	42	43	44	45	46	47	48	49	50
51	52	53	54	55	56	57	58	59	60
61	62	63	64	65	66	67	68	69	70
71	72	73	74	75	76	77	78	79	80
81	82	83	84	85	86	87	88	89	90
91	92	93	94	95	96	97	98	99	100

Challenge 1

1 Colour 10 more than 30. **2** Colour 10 more than 25.

Challenge 2

1 a Colour 10 more than 9. **b** Colour 10 less than 68.

2 Count on or back in 10s to find:

a 10 more than 54 ⬚ **b** 10 more than 40 ⬚

c 10 less than 22 ⬚ **d** 10 more than 33 ⬚

Challenge 3

Count on or back in 10s to find:

1 20 more than 9 ⬚ **2** 30 more than 37 ⬚

3 20 less than 61 ⬚ **4** 40 less than 52 ⬚

Lesson 1: **Addition and subtraction number bonds for 10 (2)**

• Know addition and subtraction number bonds for 10

Challenge 1   Complete the number sentence.

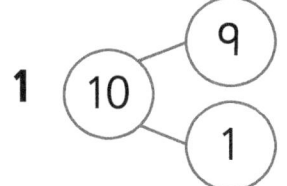

1 10 — 9, 1

2 10 — 5, 5

9 + ☐ = 10

☐ + ☐ = 10

Challenge 2   **1** Complete the number sentences for each bond.

a 10 — 8, 2

☐ + ☐ = 10   ☐ − ☐ = 2

b 10 — 4, 6

☐ + ☐ = 10   ☐ − ☐ = 6

2 Use the same numbers to write another number sentence.

a 7 + 3 = 10   ☐ + ☐ = 10

b 10 − 7 = 3   10 − ☐ = ☐

Challenge 3   Write two additions and two subtractions.

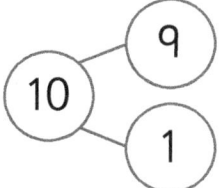

10 — 9, 1

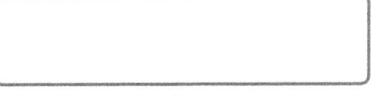

Lesson 2: **Addition and subtraction number bonds**

• Write addition and subtraction number bonds to 10

Number

Challenge 1 Complete the addition number bonds for 5.

4 + ☐ = 5   3 + ☐ = 5

Challenge 2 **1** Complete the addition number bonds for 7.

2 + ☐ = 7   3 + ☐ = 7   5 + ☐ = 7

2 Write three subtraction number bonds for 7.

7 – ☐ = ☐   7 – ☐ = ☐   7 – ☐ = ☐

3 Write three addition number bonds for 6.

☐ + ☐ = 6   ☐ + ☐ = 6   ☐ + ☐ = 6

4 Write three subtraction number bonds for 6.

6 – ☐ = ☐   6 – ☐ = ☐   6 – ☐ = ☐

Challenge 3 **1** Write four addition number bonds for 9.

☐ + ☐ = 9   ☐ + ☐ = 9

☐ + ☐ = 9   ☐ + ☐ = 9

2 Write four subtraction number bonds for 9.

9 – ☐ = ☐   9 – ☐ = ☐

9 – ☐ = ☐   9 – ☐ = ☐

Lesson 3: **Adding two single-digit numbers (2)**

• Add single-digit numbers together

Number

Challenge 1 Make 10 and then count on to add.

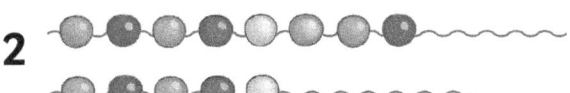

1   9 + 3 = ☐

2   8 + 5 = ☐

Challenge 2 Make 10 and then count on to add.

1

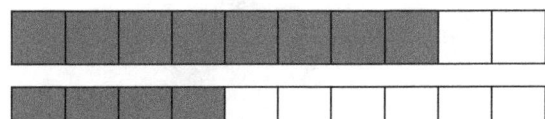

8 + 4 = ☐

2

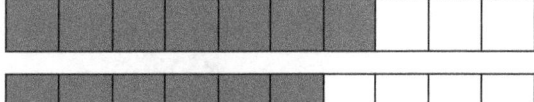

7 + 6 = ☐

3

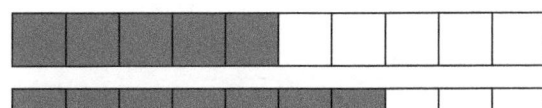

5 + 7 = ☐

4

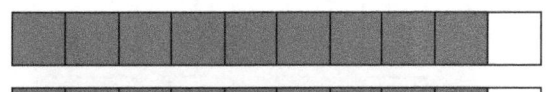

9 + 9 = ☐

Challenge 3 Make 10 and then count on to add.
Use the 10s frame to help you.

1 8 + 6 = ☐

2 5 + 9 = ☐

Number

• Add two numbers by putting the larger
  number first and counting on

Challenge
1
Find the larger number, then count on to add the
numbers together.

1 ☐

 1   7

2 ☐

 2   9

Challenge
2
Rewrite these additions, putting the larger number first.
Count on to find the answer.

1 3 + 8 = ☐ + ☐ = ☐

2 4 + 9 = ☐ + ☐ = ☐

3 2 + 6 = ☐ + ☐ = ☐

Challenge
3
Use numbers from the box to write additions.
Put the larger number first and count on to find the answer.

10	2	7	5	9	3

☐ + ☐ = ☐   ☐ + ☐ = ☐

☐ + ☐ = ☐   ☐ + ☐ = ☐

Lesson 5: **Missing number calculations**: addition

• Find the missing number in an addition

Challenge 1   Draw the missing triangles.

1 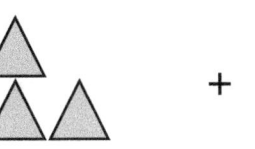 + [   ] =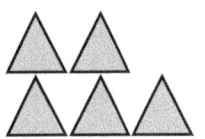

2 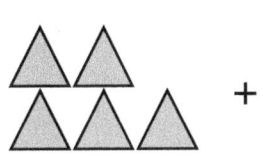 + [   ] =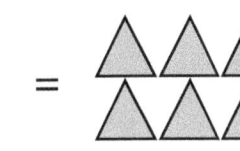

Challenge 2   Write the missing numbers.

1  8 + [ ] = 10 **2** 5 + [ ] = 9

3 [ ] + 5 = 8 **4** 3 + [ ] = 7

5 [ ] + 4 = 8 **6** 4 + [ ] = 9

Challenge 3   Write the missing numbers.

1 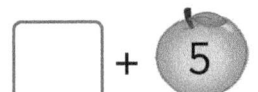 7 + [ ] =  13 **2** [ ] +  10 = 15

3 [ ] + 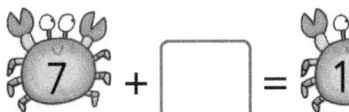 12 = 19 **4** 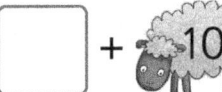 11 + [ ] =  29

Lesson 6: **Missing number calculations**: subtraction

• Find the missing number in a subtraction

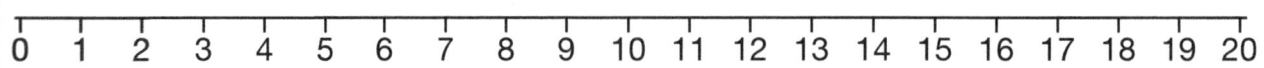

Challenge 1 Find the missing numbers. Use the number line to help you.

1 ☐ – 4 = 2   **2** ☐ – 3 = 7

3 6 – ☐ = 3   **4** 5 – ☐ = 1

Challenge 2 Write the missing numbers. Use the number line to help you.

1 10 – ☐ = 8   **2** 8 – ☐ = 7

3 ☐ – 6 = 3   **4** 5 – ☐ = 5

5 ☐ – 3 = 4   **6** 6 – ☐ = 4

Challenge 3 Lily made 10 cakes. Her dad ate some of them. There were 7 cakes left.

1 How many cakes did Lily's dad eat?
Use the number line to help you. ☐

 – ? =

2 Write the number sentence. ☐ ◯ ☐ = ☐

Lesson 7: **Adding single- and 2-digit numbers (1)**

- Add single- and 2-digit numbers

Number

Challenge 1 Count on to find the answer.

1 13 + = ☐

2 15 + ★★ = ☐

3 11 + = ☐

1	2	3	4	5	6	7	8	9	10
11	12	13	14	15	16	17	18	19	20
21	22	23	24	25	26	27	28	29	30
31	32	33	34	35	36	37	38	39	40
41	42	43	44	45	46	47	48	49	50
51	52	53	54	55	56	57	58	59	60
61	62	63	64	65	66	67	68	69	70
71	72	73	74	75	76	77	78	79	80
81	82	83	84	85	86	87	88	89	90
91	92	93	94	95	96	97	98	99	100

Challenge 2 Find the larger number and count on.

1 18 + 4 =

2 43 + 7 =

3 2 + 39 =

4 8 + 71 =

Challenge 3 Find the larger number and count on.

1 47 + 5 =

2 8 + 25 =

3 9 + 74 =

4 66 + 6 =

5 86 + 7 =

6 4 + 88 =

53

Lesson 8: **Adding single- and 2-digit numbers (2)**

• Solve word problems by adding single- and 2-digit numbers

Number

Challenge 1

1 Joe finds 15 shells. He has 3 more at home. How many shells does he have now?

◻ + ◻ = ◻

2 Louise makes 12 biscuits. There are 4 more in the tin. How many biscuits are there?

◻ + ◻ = ◻

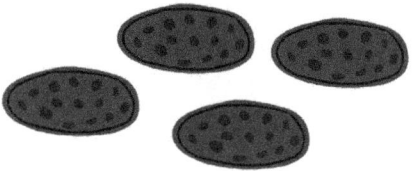

Challenge 2

1 Henry has 23 marbles. Josh has 6 marbles. How many marbles do they have altogether?

◻ + ◻ = ◻

2 Bella picks 32 flowers. James picks 5 flowers. How many flowers do they have altogether?

◻ + ◻ = ◻

Challenge 3

1 Jane has 5 pet mice. They have 18 babies. How many mice does she have now?

◻ + ◻ = ◻

2 There are 87 children in the school. 9 new children join.

◻ + ◻ = ◻

How many children go to the school now?

Lesson 1: **Doubles to 5**

• Find and make doubles for the numbers to 5

Challenge 1 Draw the same number of dots again to make double the amount.

1 ● ● ● [ ]

2 ● [ ]

3 ● ● [ ]

4 ● ● ● ● ● [ ]

Challenge 2 Draw the same number of spots on the ladybirds to make double the amount.

1

Double 4 = [ ]

2

Double 5 = [ ]

3

Double 1 = [ ]

4

Double 2 = [ ]

5

Double 3 = [ ]

6

Double 6 = [ ]

Challenge 3 Draw lines to match each number to its double.

 2   12

 4   6

 6   4

 3   8

55

Lesson 2: **Groups of 2 (1)**

Number

• Make groups of 2
• Start to recognise multiples of 2

Challenge 1 Fill in the blanks.

1

⬜ groups of 2. ⬜ cubes altogether.

2

⬜ groups of 2. ⬜ cubes altogether.

Challenge 2 How many altogether? Draw dots on the leaves to help you.

1 4 groups of 2 = ⬜

2 1 group of 2 = ⬜

3 5 groups of 2 = ⬜

Challenge 3 How many groups of 2 can you make from these amounts?

1 12 = ⬜ groups of 2   **2** 16 = ⬜ groups of 2

Lesson 3: **Groups of 2 (2)**

• Recognise multiples of 2

You will need
• coloured pencils

Challenge 1 Colour the multiples of 2.

1	2	3	4	5	6	7	8	9	10
11	12	13	14	15	16	17	18	19	20

Challenge 2 **1** Circle all the multiples of 2.

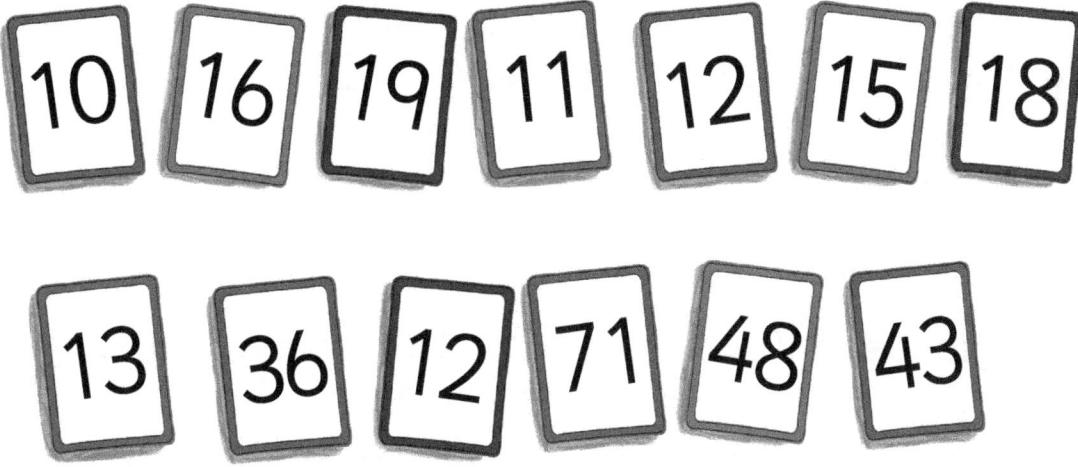

10 16 19 11 12 15 18

13 36 12 71 48 43

2 Write some more multiples of 2.

Challenge 3 Write five multiples of 2 greater than 50.

57

Lesson 4: **Groups of 10 (1)**

Number

> • Make groups of 10
> • Start to recognise multiples of 10

Challenge 1 Fill in the blanks.

1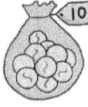

☐ groups of 10. ☐ marbles altogether.

2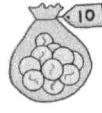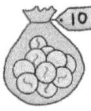

☐ groups of 10. ☐ marbles altogether.

Challenge 2 How many altogether?

1 8 groups of 10 = ☐   **2** 3 groups of 10 = ☐

3 7 groups of 10 = ☐   **4** 10 groups of 10 = ☐

Challenge 3

1 7 children have been collecting shells.
They have 10 shells each.
How many shells is that altogether? ☐

2 You can have 10 turns at the game at the fair for $1.
Joe pays $5. How many turns can he have? ☐

$1 = 10. $5 = ?

Number

- Recognise multiples of 10

You will need
- coloured pencils

Challenge 1 Fill in the missing numbers.
Colour the multiples of 10.

| 1 | 2 | 3 | 4 | 5 | | 7 | 8 | 9 | | 11 | 12 | 13 | 14 | 15 | 16 |

33		31		29	28	27	26		24	23	22			19	18
34															
35	36		38	39		41	42	43		45	46	47			

| | | | | | | | | | | | | | | | 51 |

| | 66 | 65 | 64 | | 62 | 61 | | 59 | | | 56 | 55 | 54 | 53 | 52 |

69		71		73	74	75	76		78	79		81	82	83	
															85

| 100 | | 98 | 97 | 96 | | 94 | 93 | 92 | 91 | | 89 | | 87 | |

Challenge 2 Circle the multiples of 10.

60   51   100   92   30   70   33   20

55   90   35   10   80

Challenge 3 Tick (✓) the multiples of 10.

300 ☐   680 ☐   725 ☐   410 ☐

How do you know?

_____

_____

☹ 😐 ☺

Lesson 6: **Sharing objects into 2 equal groups (1)**

- Share objects into 2 equal groups

You will need
- 20 counters

 Challenge 1 Ahmed is sharing 10 strawberries with a friend. Is it fair? Write yes or no.

1

2

Challenge 2 Use counters to count out the numbers. Share them into two equal groups. How many counters are in each group?

1 4 ☐   **2** 2 ☐   **3** 8 ☐

4 10 ☐   **5** 6 ☐   **6** 12 ☐

 Challenge 3

1 Mahira wants to share 16 grapes with her friend. How many grapes will they have each? ☐

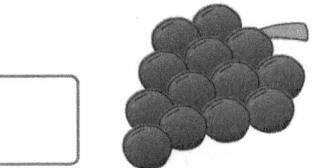

2 Sayed wants to share 20 pieces of mango with his dad. How many pieces of mango will they have each? ☐

Lesson 7: **Sharing objects into 2 equal groups (2)**

• Share objects into 2 equal groups

You will need
• 20 counters

 Use counters to share out the number between the bears.

1  4

2  6

☐ ☐

☐ ☐

Challenge 2 Share each number into 2 groups. How many counters in each group?

 8   6   10   2

Challenge 3 Tick the lines that will share equally between 2 groups.

1 ○○○○○○○○○○

2 ○○○○○○○○○○○○

3 ○○○○○○○○○○○○○○○○○○○○○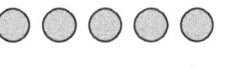

61

Lesson 8: **Problems involving grouping and sharing (1)**

- Solve problems by making groups or sharing

You will need
- 20 counters
- 2 toys

Challenge 1 Share the cookies into 2 groups. Circle the groups.

1 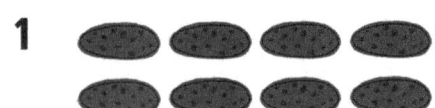   2

Challenge 2 Share the strawberries. Draw them on the plates.

1    2

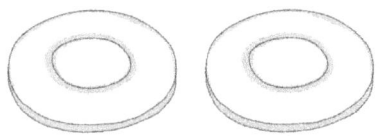   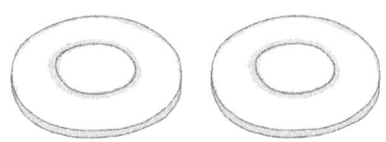

[ ] shared between 2 is [ ]   [ ] shared between 2 is [ ]

Challenge 3 Share the party food.

1 Hiro has [ ] cakes.

He shares them with Ronan.

They have [ ] cakes each.

2 Jasmin has [ ] sweets.

She shares them equally with Laura.

They have [ ] sweets each.

Lesson 1: **Doubles to 10**

Number

• Find and make doubles for the numbers to 10

Challenge 1 Draw the same amount to make double.

1

Double 4 = ☐

2

Double 3 = ☐

Challenge 2 Draw the same amount to make double.

1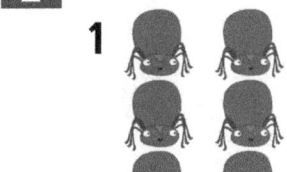

Double 7 = ☐

2

Double 6 = ☐

3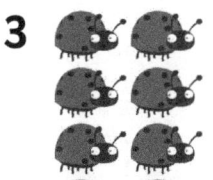

Double 10 = ☐

4

Double 8 = ☐

Challenge 3 Circle the number that is double the star number.

7 7   10   14   12   11

10 18   25   15   20   10

9 16   12   14   20   18

11 2   22   51   30   12

8 15   9   16   18   20

25 7   70   25   50   30

☹
😐
☺

Lesson 2: **Near doubles**

Number

• Solve additions by finding near doubles

Challenge 1

Complete the 'double + 1' calculations.

1 2 + 2 = ☐ so 2 + 3 = ☐

2 7 + 7 = ☐ so 7 + 8 = ☐

Challenge 2

Use doubling to work out the answers.

1 3 + 4 = ?

Double ☐3☐ = ☐6☐

☐6☐ (+) ☐1☐ = ☐7☐

2 6 + 7 = ?

Double ☐ = ☐

☐ ◯ ☐ = ☐

3 8 + 9 = ?

Double ☐ = ☐

☐ ◯ ☐ = ☐

4 9 + 10 = ?

Double ☐ = ☐

☐ ◯ ☐ = ☐

Challenge 3

Use doubling to work out the answers.

1 13 + 14 = ?

Double ☐ = ☐   ☐ ◯ ☐ = ☐

2 11 + 12 = ?

Double ☐ = ☐   ☐ ◯ ☐ = ☐

Lesson 3: **Groups of 2 (3)**

• Recognise multiples of 2

Challenge 1
Join the multiples of 2, in order, to make a picture. Start on 2.

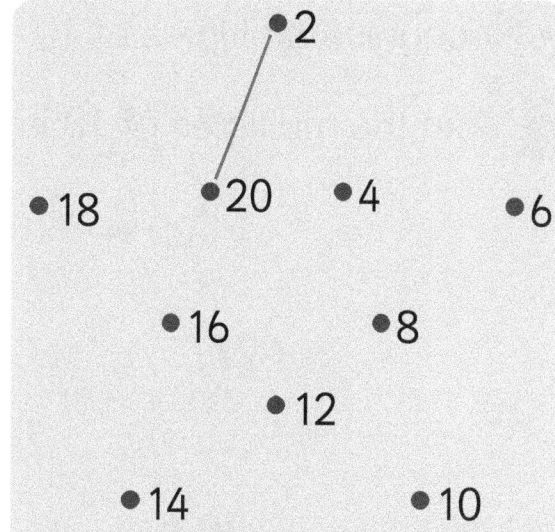

Challenge 2
Join the multiples of 2, in order, to make a picture. Start on 2.

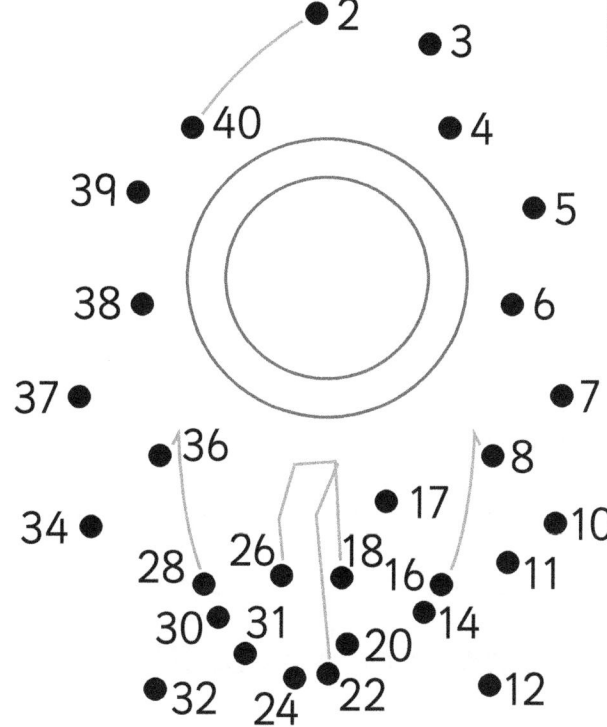

Challenge 3

1 Write three multiples of 2 between 50 and 80.

2 Write three multiples of 2 between 80 and 100.

Lesson 4: **Groups of 10 (3)**

• Recognise multiples of 10

Challenge 1 Join the multiples of 10 in order to make a number.

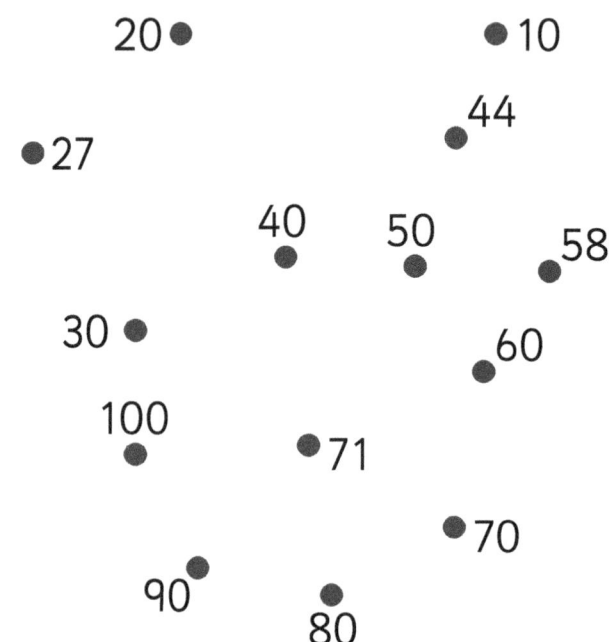

20•   •10
                 •44
•27
        40   50
         •   •   •58
30 •
                  •60
  100
    •   •71

                  •70
   90•
      •80

Challenge 2 **1** Fill in the missing multiples of 10.

10

2 Circle the numbers that are **not** multiples of 10.

20   70   41   80   91   90   40   16   30

Challenge 3 Circle the multiples of 2. Cross out the multiples of 10.

10   64   80   42   40   37   96   60   73   20   ☹

                                                     😐

What do you notice about some of the numbers?   😊

Lesson 5: **Sharing objects into 2 equal groups (3)**

• Share objects into 2 equal groups

Challenge 1 Tick the sets that have been shared equally.

1 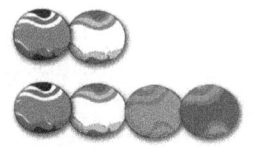 ☐

2  ☐

3  ☐

4  ☐

Challenge 2 Share the numbers equally. Draw dots in the boxes.

1 8

2 14

3 18

4 10

Challenge 3

1 Share 8 stickers with your friend.
How many do you have each? ☐

2 Share 12 pencils equally between 2 pencil cases.
How many pencils are in each case? ☐

Lesson 6: **Sharing numbers to 10**

Number

• Work out if a number is odd or even by sharing it between 2

Challenge 1

Odd or even? Circle the answer.

1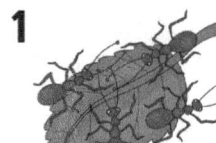

odd   even

2

odd   even

Challenge 2

Draw dots for each number. Share them between 2 boxes. Is each number odd or even? Circle the answer.

1 ⭐ 6

odd   even

2 ⭐ 7

odd   even

3 ⭐ 9

odd   even

4 ⭐ 4

odd   even

Challenge 3

Draw dots for each number. Share them between 2 boxes. Is each number odd or even? Circle the answer.

1 ⭐ 15

odd   even

2 ⭐ 18

odd   even

Lesson 7: **Halves**

Number

• Find half of an even number by sharing into 2 equal groups

 Challenge 1 Count the spots on one side of the ladybird to find half.

1

2

Half of 4 is ☐ .

Half of 6 is ☐ .

 Challenge 2 Draw spots equally on both sides. Count the spots on one side to find half.

1 Half of 4 is ☐ .

2 Half of 2 is ☐ .

3 Half of 8 is ☐ .

4 Half of 10 is ☐ .

Challenge 3 Circle true or false.

1 Half of 12 is 6.

true   false

2 Half of 14 is 8.

true   false

Lesson 8: **Problems involving grouping and sharing (2)**

• Solve problems by making groups or sharing

Challenge 1 Lana shares 6 flowers equally between 2 friends.

How many flowers do they each get? ▢

Challenge 2 **1** 2 horses ate a total of 10 apples. They each ate the same number of apples.

How many apples did each horse eat? ▢

2 Circle the answer.

a Maya has 7 toy animals to share with her sister.

Can she share them equally?   yes   no

b Is 7 an odd or an even number?   odd   even

Challenge 3 Dan wants to buy nuts to share equally with Tom.

Should Dan buy 13, 14 or 15 nuts? ▢

Why?

_____

Lesson 1: **Naming 2D shapes**

- Recognise and name circles, triangles, rectangles and squares

You will need
- red, blue, purple and green coloured pencils

Geometry

Challenge 1 Match the same shapes.

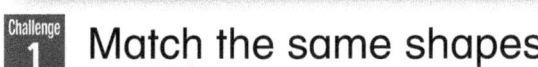

Challenge 2 Colour the shapes in the house.

triangles   blue   circles   red

squares   green   rectangles   purple

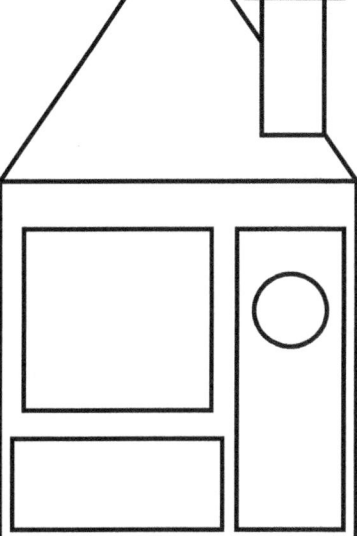

Challenge 3 Colour.

triangles   blue   circles   red

squares   green   rectangles   purple

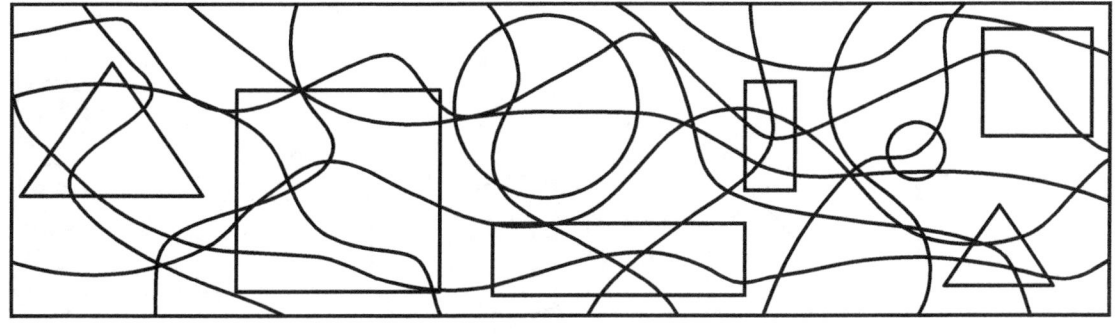

Lesson 2: **Sorting 2D shapes**

Geometry

- Sort circles, squares, rectangles and triangles

You will need
- coloured pencils

Challenge 1 Colour the shapes that are the same.

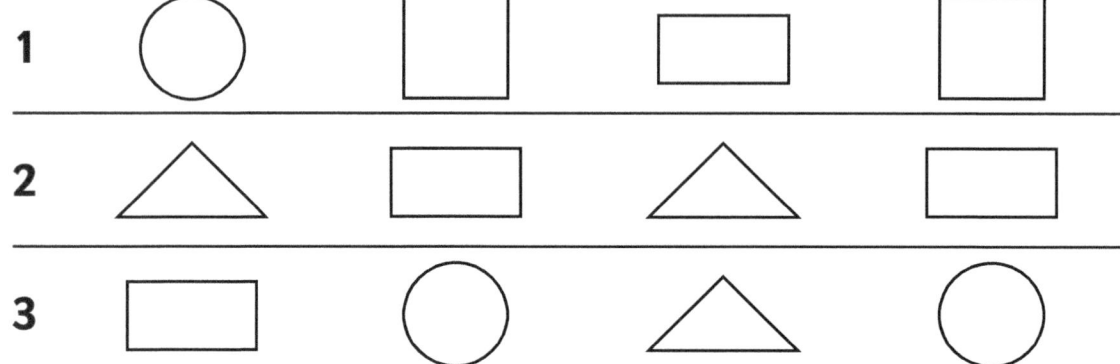

1

2

3

Challenge 2 Join the balloons to the right shape.

square   rectangle   triangle   circle

Challenge 3 Draw lines to show how many sides.

| 1 side | 3 sides | 4 sides |

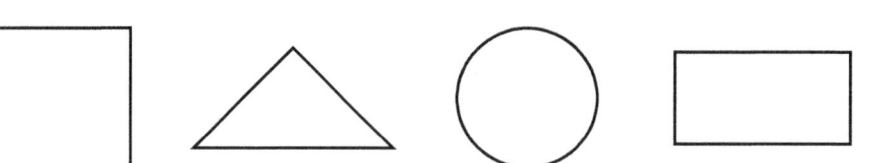

Lesson 3: **Describing 2D shapes**

Geometry

- Recognise the features of circles, triangles, rectangles and squares

You will need
- coloured pencils

Challenge 1 Trace and count the sides.

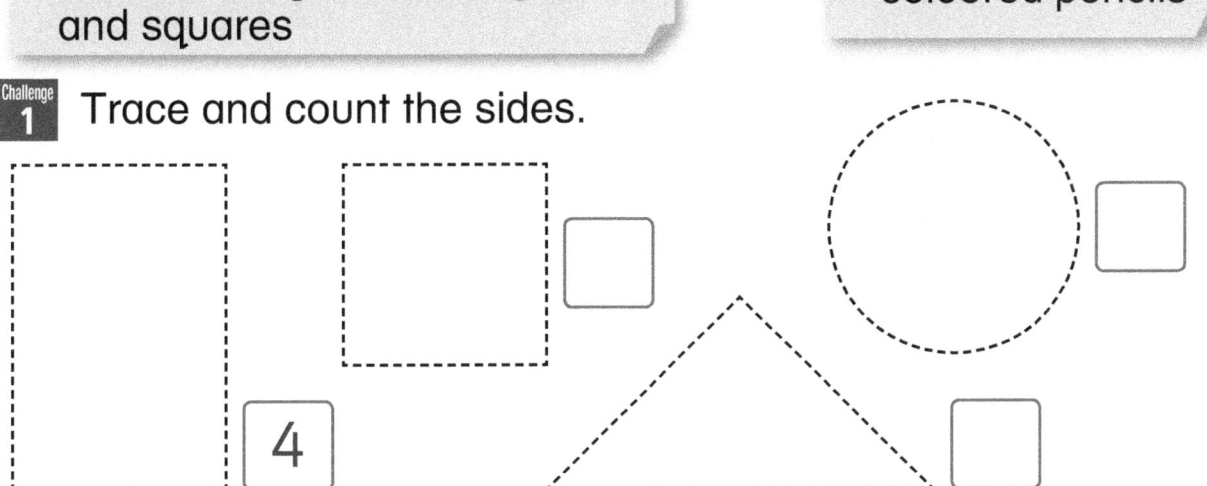

4

Challenge 2 Join the shapes to the right box.

curved side

4 sides

3 corners

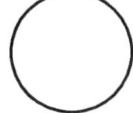

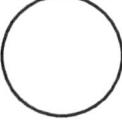

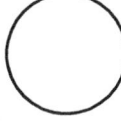

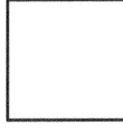

Challenge 3 Colour the shapes that have both curved **and** straight sides.

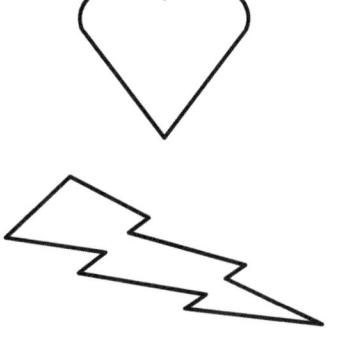

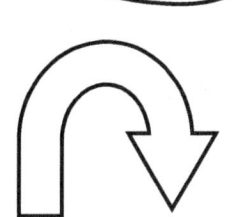
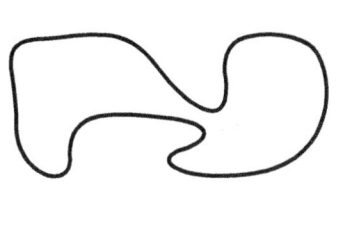

Lesson 4: **Making patterns using 2D shapes**

Geometry

• Make patterns using 2D shapes and talk about them

Challenge 1 Draw a pattern made of shapes.

Challenge 2 Draw the next shapes in each pattern.

1

2

3

Challenge 3 Draw the next shapes in the pattern.

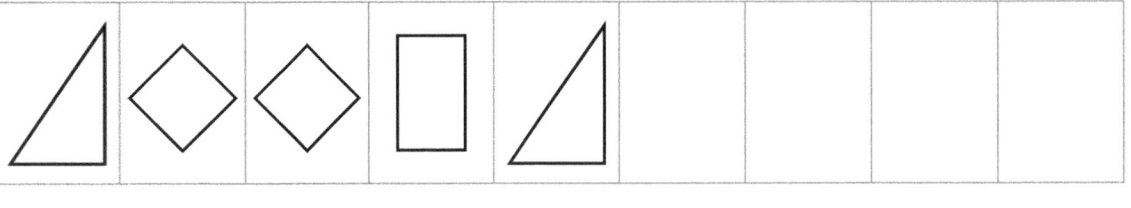

Lesson 1: **Naming 3D shapes**

• Recognise and name spheres, cones, cylinders, cubes and cuboids

You will need
• coloured pencils

 Trace the words.

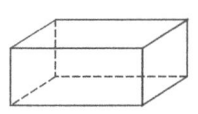 cuboid

cube

 sphere

cylinder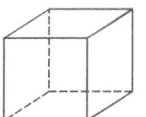

cone

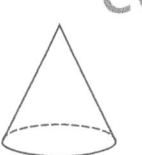

Challenge 2 Colour the 3D shapes.

Challenge 3 Join each shape to its name.

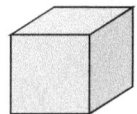   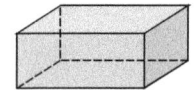   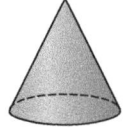   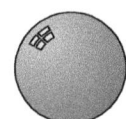   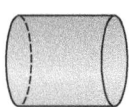

cone   sphere   cuboid   cylinder   cube

75

Lesson 2: **Sorting 3D shapes**

* Sort spheres, cones, cylinders, cubes and cuboids

Geometry

Challenge 1 Circle the curved shapes.

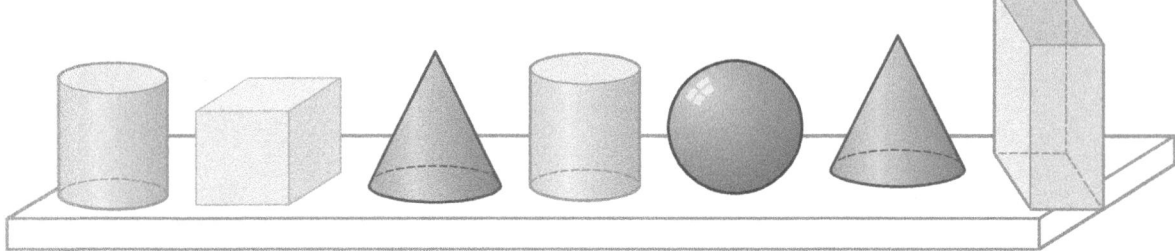

Challenge 2 Do these shapes roll? ✓ for yes, ✗ for no.

cylinder

cube

sphere

cuboid

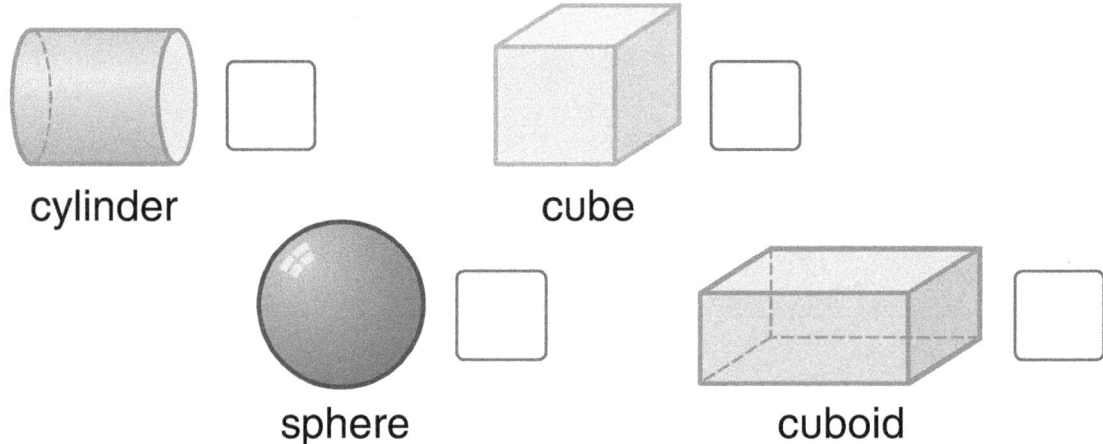

Challenge 3 Join the objects to the same shape.

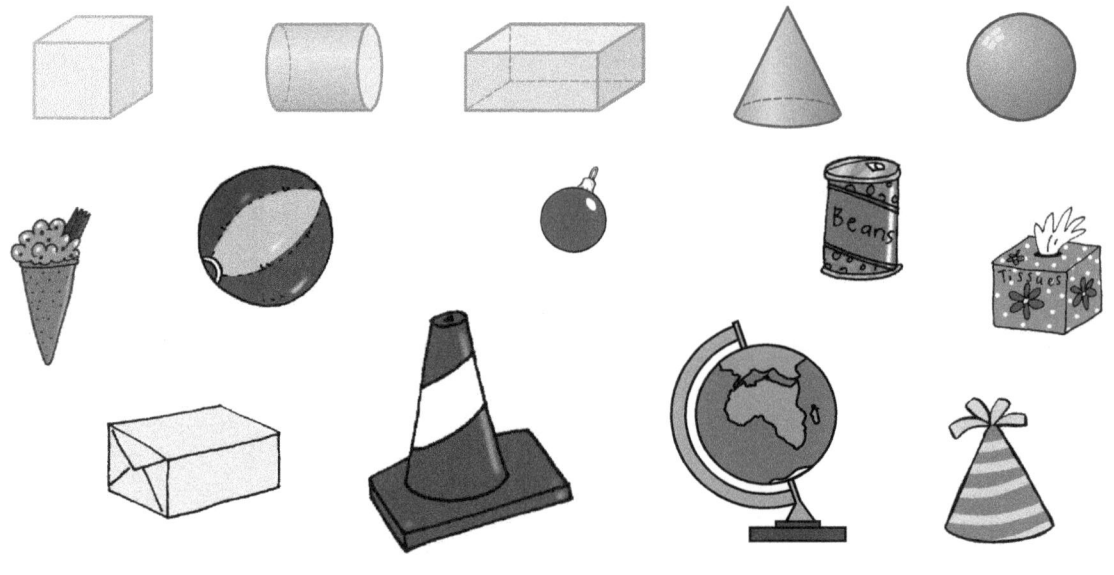

Lesson 3: **Describing 3D shapes**

• Recognise the features of spheres, cones, cylinders, cubes and cuboids

You will need
• coloured pencils

Challenge 1 Colour the shapes with 6 flat faces.

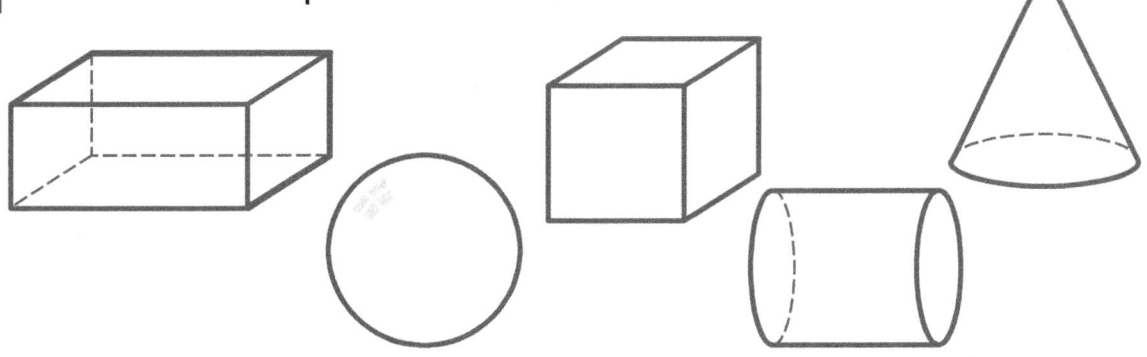

Challenge 2 Match each picture to the number of faces and the description.

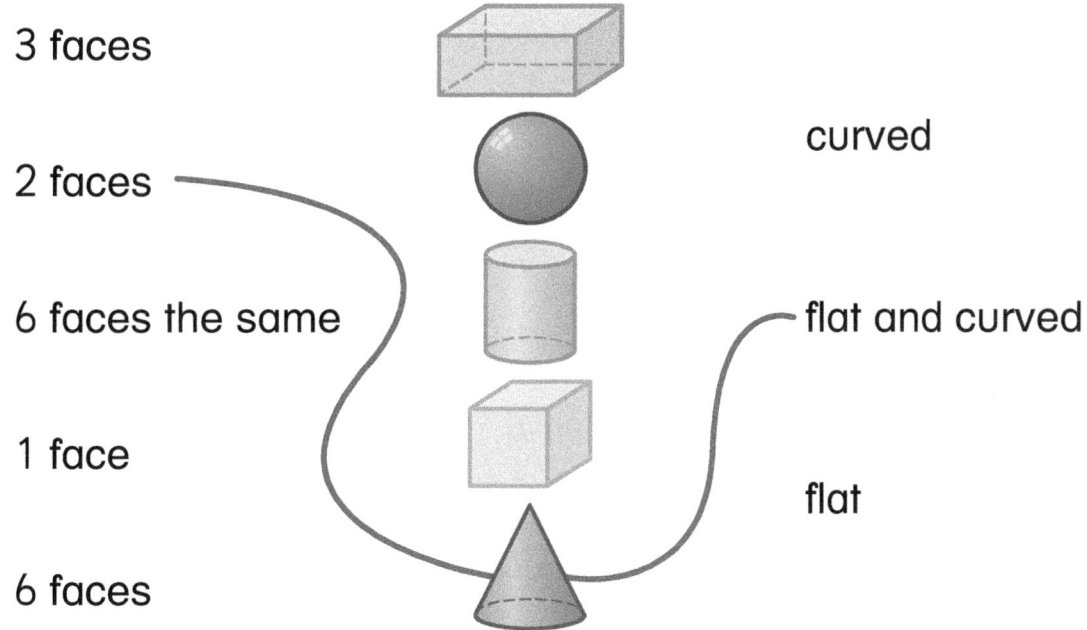

3 faces

2 faces

6 faces the same

1 face

6 faces

curved

flat and curved

flat

Challenge 3 Circle the shape with 6 faces the same.

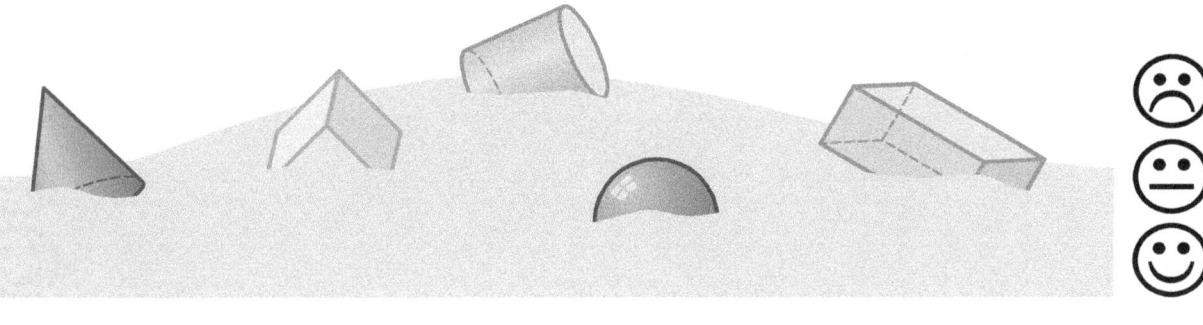

Lesson 4: **Making patterns using 3D shapes**

- Make patterns using spheres, cones, cylinders, cubes and cuboids

Challenge 1 Draw the next 3 shapes in each pattern.

1
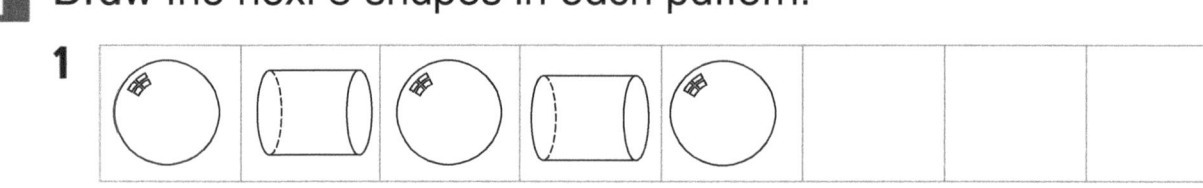

2

Challenge 2 Draw the next 4 shapes in each pattern.

1
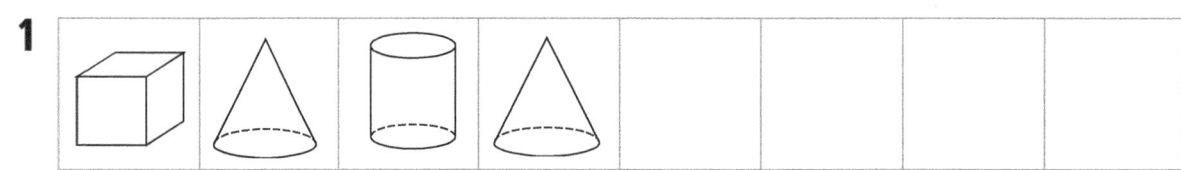

2

Challenge 3 Choose 3 shapes. Make a pattern.

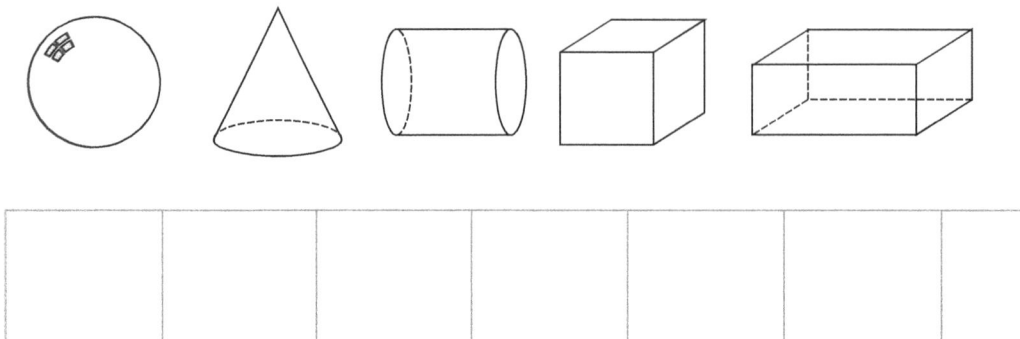

Lesson 1: **Recognising symmetry**

- Recognise symmetry in the world around us

You will need
- coloured pencils

Challenge 1 Colour the rainbow so both sides match.

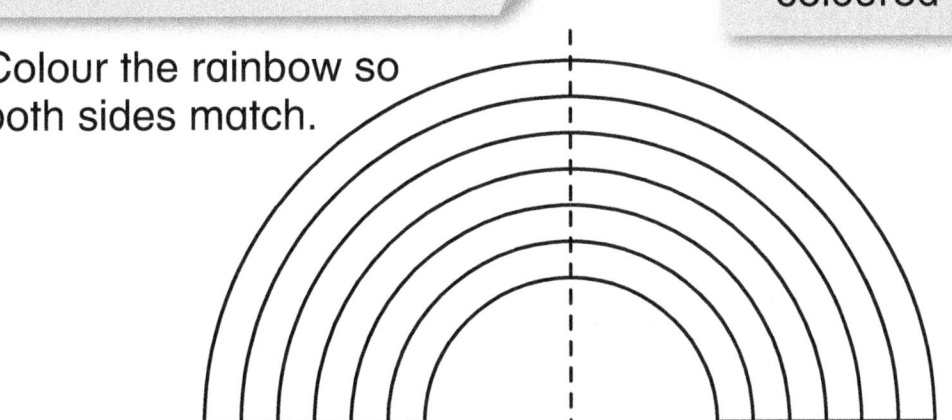

Challenge 2 **1** Colour the matching halves the same colour.

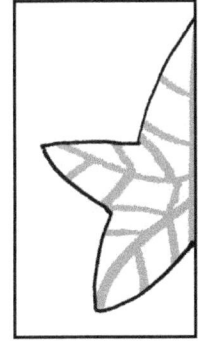  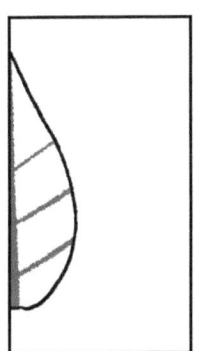  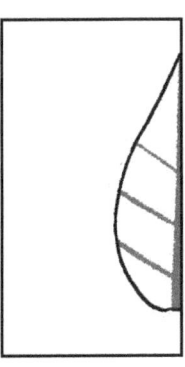 

2 Tick the images that show symmetry.

Challenge 3 Draw a mirror image of the shape.

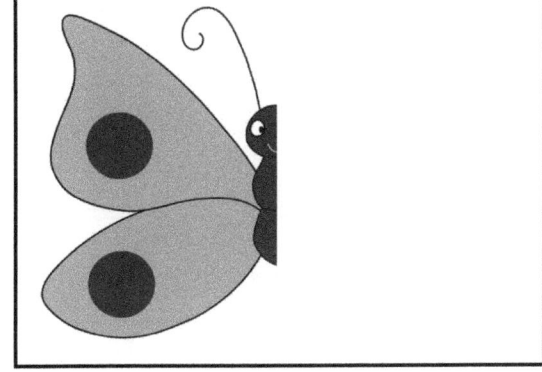

Geometry

• Find lines of symmetry in 2D shapes

Challenge 1 Circle the correct line of symmetry.

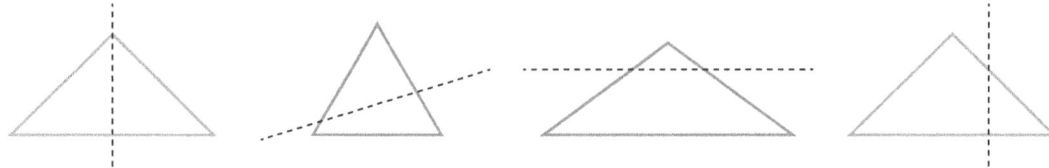

Challenge 2 Draw lines of symmetry.

Challenge 3 Draw lines of symmetry.

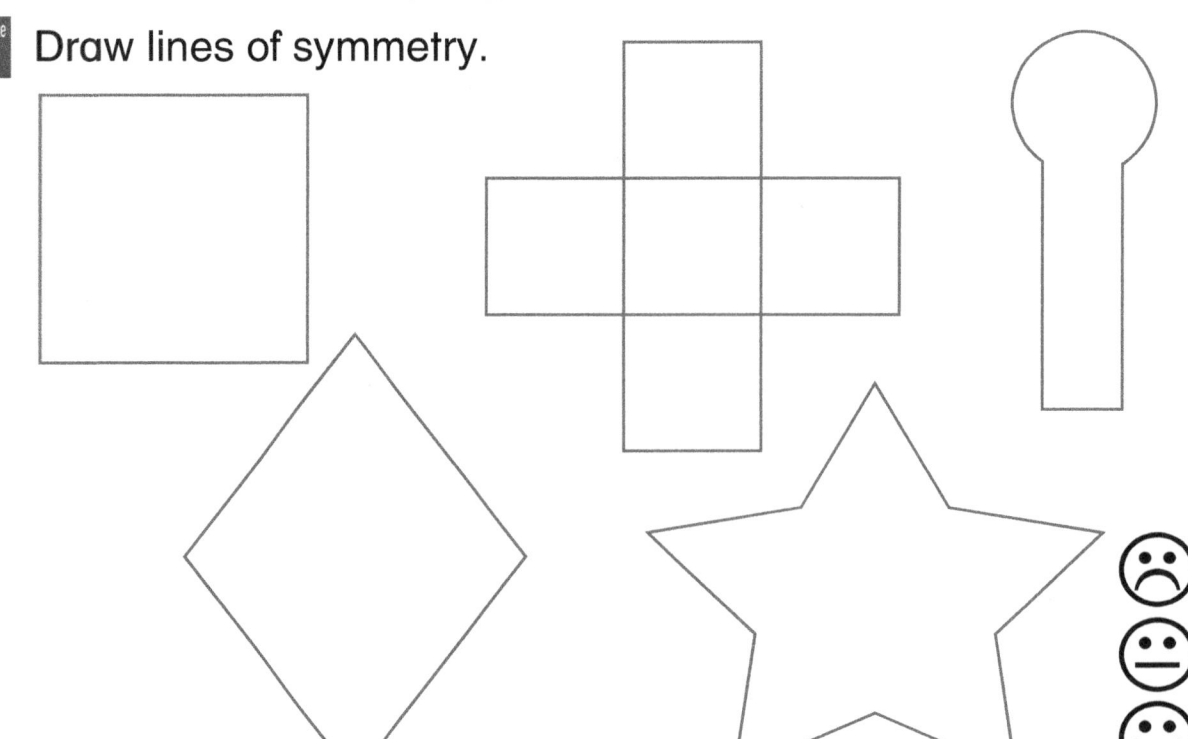

Lesson 3: **Making symmetrical shapes**

- Make symmetrical shapes and talk about them

You will need
- coloured pencils

 Make a symmetrical shape.

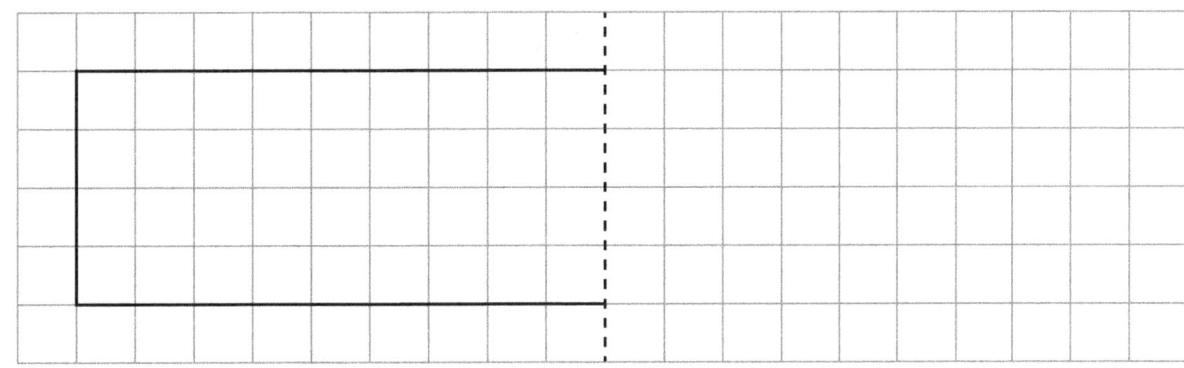

 Challenge 2 Make a symmetrical shape.

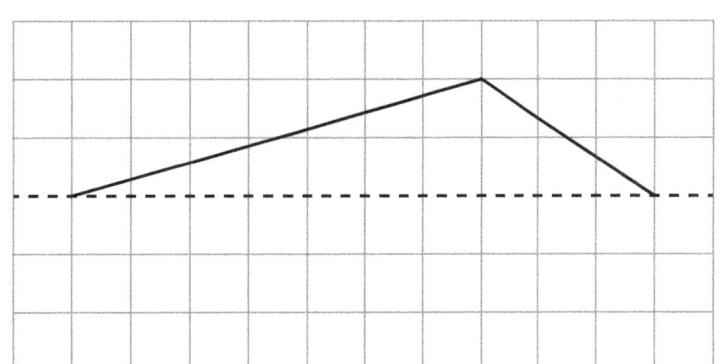

Challenge 3 Shade squares to make a symmetrical shape.

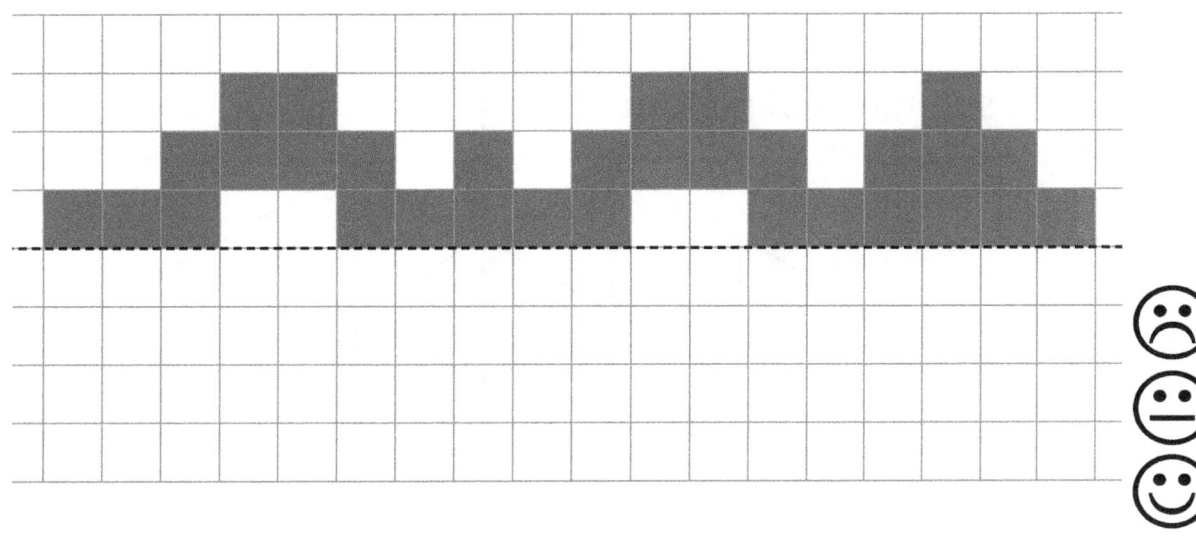

Lesson 4: **Making symmetrical patterns**

Geometry

- Make symmetrical patterns and talk about them

You will need
- coloured pencils
- small mirror

Challenge 1

1. Add dots to make the picture symmetrical.

2. Colour the dots – make sure it is still symmetrical.

Challenge 2

Using a black pencil, make the pattern show symmetry.

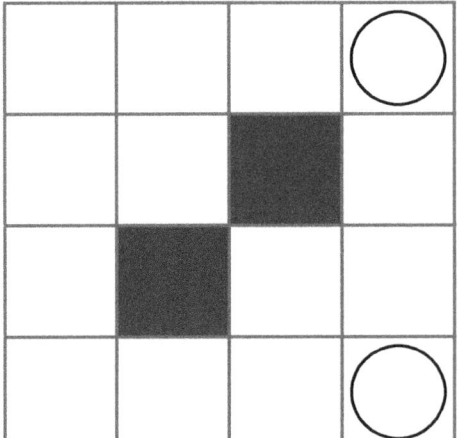

Challenge 3

Make a symmetrical pattern using two colours.

Lesson 1: **Describing direction**

Unit **13**

Geometry

• Give directions to move an object

Challenge 1 Circle the word that shows where the kite is.

up   **down**   **up**   **down**

Challenge 2 Where is Ted going? Circle the correct word.

forwards   backwards

Challenge 3 The moved **right** to the . It went **up** the

and **down** the . It moved **right** to the ⚫ and went

around it. It went **left** to the Start.

Draw the snail's journey.

START

83

Lesson 2: **Describing position**

Geometry

• Describe an object's position

You will need
• coloured pencils

Challenge 1 Draw:

   in

   on

   behind

Challenge 2 Where is the cat?

on

outside

behind

under

inside

Challenge 3 Draw:

   over

   under

   inside

   behind

Lesson 3: **Describing distance**

Geometry

• Describe the distance of an object

You will need
• coloured pencils

Challenge 1 Complete the labels to show the distance of each animal from the tree.

far   close to   near

Challenge 2 Draw:

• 2 fish close to the boat   • 2 fish far from the boat
• 2 birds around the boat

Colour the nearest  to the boat blue.

Challenge 3 Circle the child:

1 nearest to the football.   **2** furthest from the football.

Lesson 4: **Describing movement**

- Talk about how I am moving an object and where I have moved it to

You will need
- coloured pencils

Geometry

Challenge 1

Draw a line to show the snail go up, down and around the tree.

Challenge 2

Draw:

a blue dot inside the △.

a red dot near the ☺.

a circle around the ♡.

Challenge 3

1 Colour something far away and near to the boy.

2 Draw:

 over the tree.

 inside the tree.

 going around the tree ↻.

Lesson 1: **Recognising coins (1)**

Unit **14**

• Recognise 1 cent, 5 cent and 10 cent coins

Challenge 1 Circle the right coin.

Challenge 2 Match each toy to a coin.

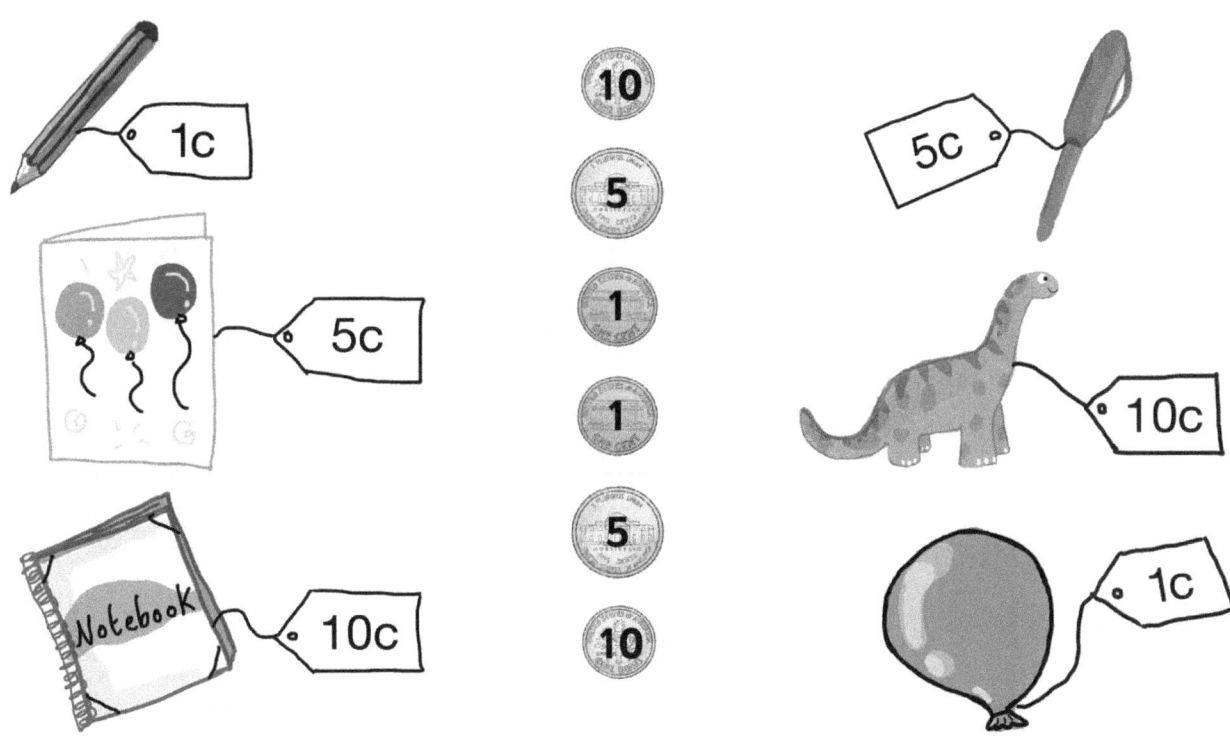

Challenge 3 Match each coin to its name.

 5 cents　　　 10 cents　　　 1 cent

Measure

Lesson 2: **Making totals (1)**

• Make totals up to 15 cents

Challenge 1 Write the total.

1  ☐ total

2  ☐ total

Challenge 2 Draw lines to match the coins with the totals.

1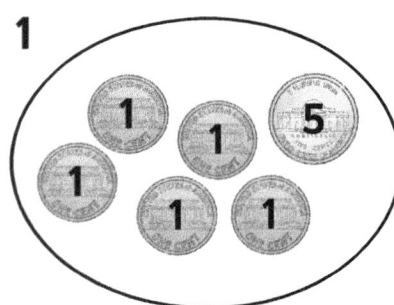

2

3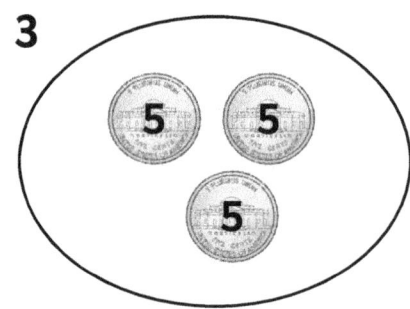

| 10c | | 15c | | 10c |

Challenge 3 Draw coins to make each total.

	Total
5 1 1	10c
10	15c
5	12c

Lesson 3: **Making equivalent totals (1)**

• Find different ways to make a total of the same value

Challenge 1 Are the amounts the same?

1   same ☐ different ☐

2   same ☐ different ☐

3 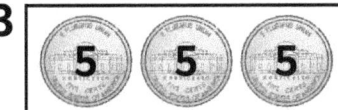  same ☐ different ☐

Challenge 2 Match each purse with the same amount.

1   2   3

Challenge 3 Show another way to make 12 cents.

Lesson 4: **Paying exact amounts (1)**

- Make a total using the smallest number of coins

Measure

Challenge 1 Draw the same amount using fewer coins.

7 cents

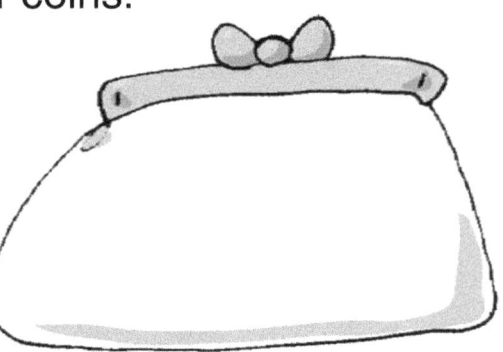

Challenge 2 Draw the smallest number of coins to make the amount.

13 cents	
6 cents	
12 cents	
14 cents	

Challenge 3 Make the same amount using fewer coins.

1 1 1 1 1 1 1 1 1 1 1 1 1 1 1	
1 1 1 1 1 5 1 1 1 1 1	

☹
😐
☺

Lesson 1: **Recognising coins (2)**

Measure

• Recognise 1 cent, 5 cent, 10 cent, 25 cent and 50 cent coins

You will need
• coloured pencils

Challenge 1 Colour:

1 cent – blue

5 cents – orange

10 cents – purple

25 cents – red

50 cents – green

Challenge 2 Circle 25c or 50c.

25 cents   50 cents   25 cents   50 cents

25 cents   50 cents   25 cents   50 cents

Challenge 3 Match each coin to its name in words.

twenty-five cents	fifty cents	ten cents

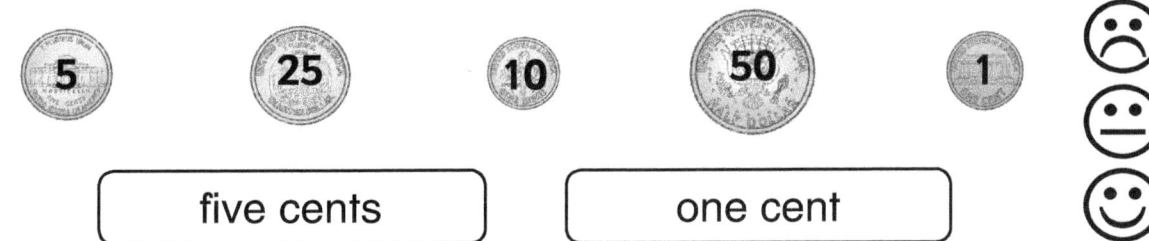

five cents	one cent

Lesson 2: **Making totals (2)**

Measure

• Make totals up to 25 cents

Challenge 1 Draw lines to match the totals.

| 10 cents | 15 cents |

Challenge 2 Draw the coins needed to make the correct total value.

16c	5 5	
25c	10 10 1	
18c	10 5	
20c	10	

Challenge 3 Draw coins to make a total value of 23 cents.

| 23c | |  |

• Find different ways to make a total of the same value

Challenge 1 Join the coins to the correct value.

1

2

| 11 cents | 13 cents |

Challenge 2 Draw different coins that make the same total.

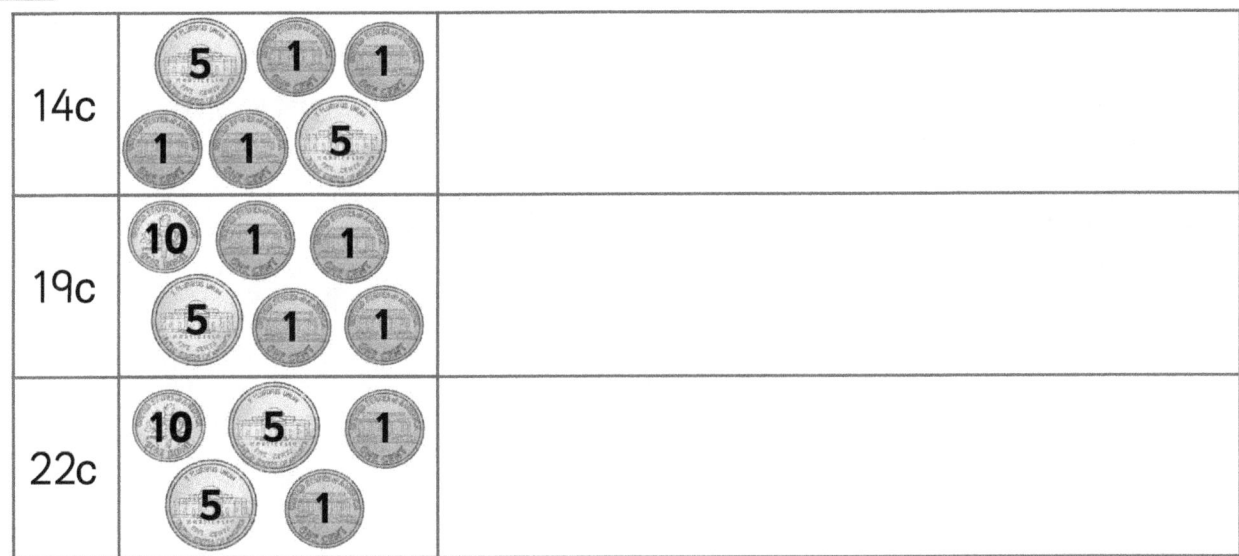

Challenge 3 Draw different coins that make the same total.

😦 😐 🙂

Lesson 4: **Paying exact amounts (2)**

• Make a total using the smallest number of coins

Challenge 1

Circle the purse with the smaller number of coins.

Challenge 2

Draw the same total value with a smaller number of coins.

I have 19 1 cent coins.

I have 17 1 cent coins.

Challenge 3

Make the amount using the smallest number of coins.

24 cents

Lesson 1: **Comparing lengths**

• Compare the length of 2 objects

Challenge 1

1 Tick the longer caterpillar.

2 Tick the shorter caterpillar.

Measure

Challenge 2

1 Draw a longer brush.

2 Draw a shorter ribbon.

Challenge 3

Circle longer or shorter.

1 Pencil A is longer / shorter than Pencil B.

2 Pencil A is longer / shorter than Pencil C.

3 Pencil B is longer / shorter than Pencil C.

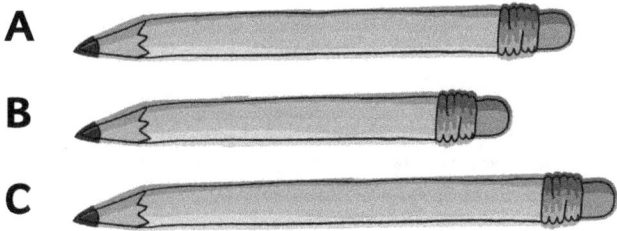

Lesson 2: **Ordering lengths**

Measure

• Order objects from shortest to longest

Challenge 1 Order the kites shortest (1) to longest (4).

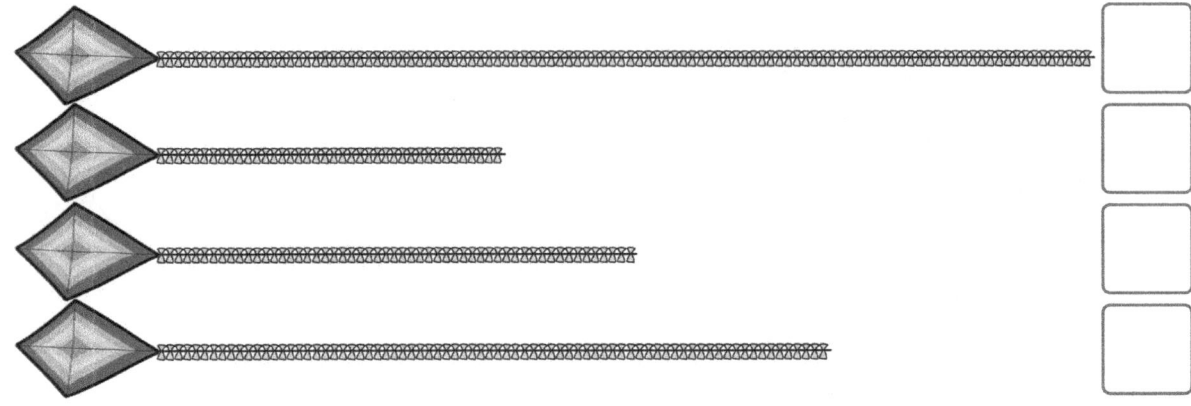

Challenge 2 Order the planes shortest (1) to longest (4).

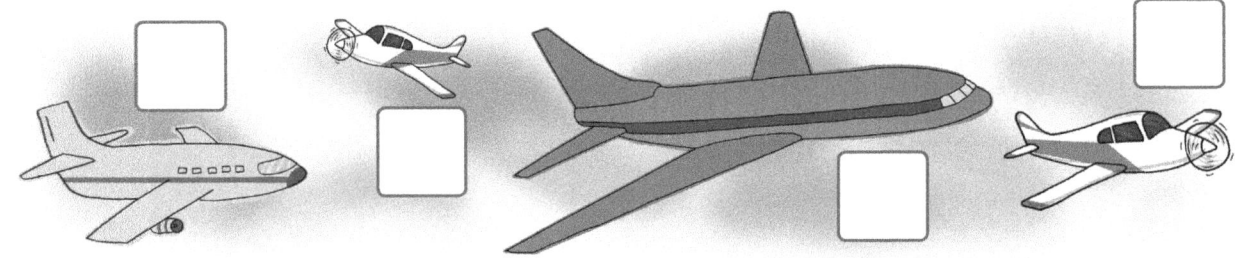

Challenge 3 Order these objects shortest (1) to longest (5).

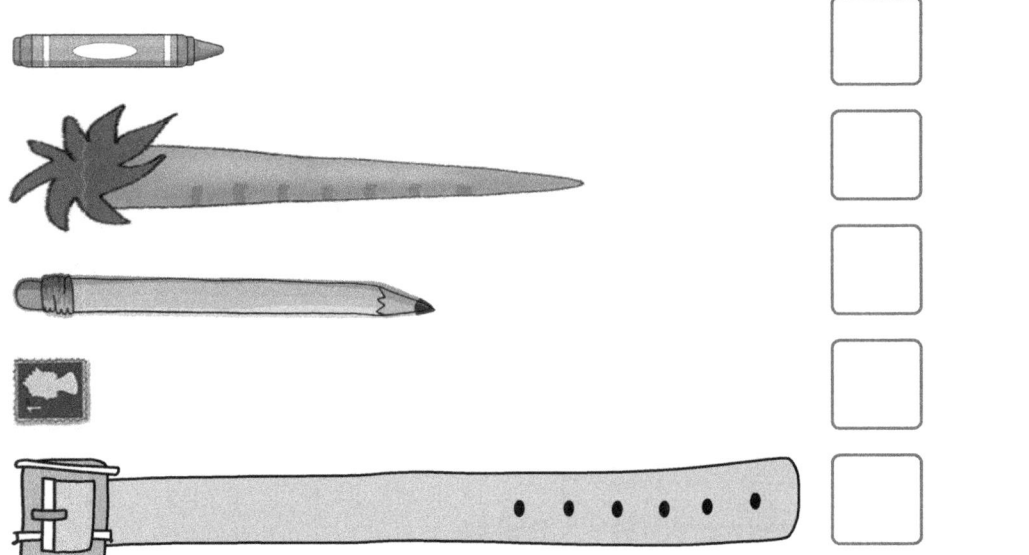

Lesson 3: **Measuring lengths**

• Measure the length of objects

You will need
• interlocking cubes
• paper clips, glue stick, crayon, pencil, notebook

Measure

Challenge 1   Use the cubes to measure.

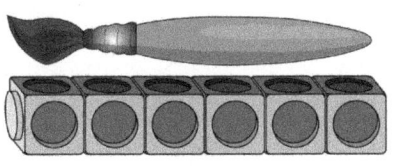

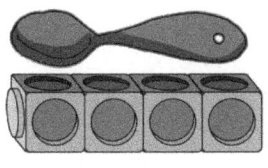

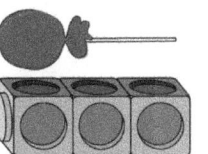

☐ cubes   ☐ cubes   ☐ cubes

Challenge 2   Use cubes to measure these things.

☐ cubes   ☐ cubes   ☐ cubes   ☐ cubes

Challenge 3   Use paper clips to measure these things.

☐ paper clips

☐ paper clips

☐ paper clips

☐ paper clips

97

Lesson 4: **Comparing height and width**

• Compare the height and the width of objects

Challenge 1 Circle the cone piled highest with ice cream.

Challenge 2

1 Circle the highest balloon.

2 Tick the widest balloon.

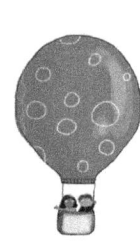  

Challenge 3 Draw a tree that is taller and with a wider trunk.

Lesson 1: **Comparing and describing weight**

- Compare the weight of 2 objects

Challenge 1 Join each animal to the right word.

heavier

lighter

Challenge 2 Tick two heavier items.

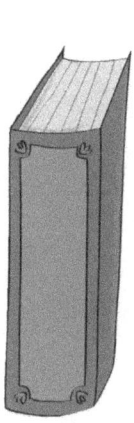
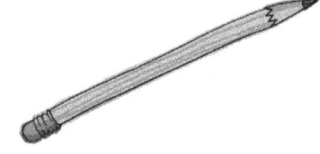

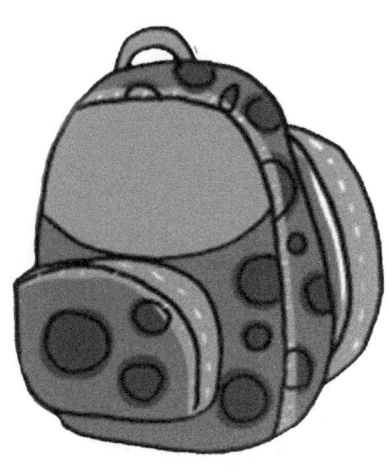

Challenge 3 Circle the right word.

1 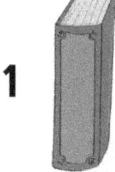 heavier / lighter than  ?

2 heavier / lighter than 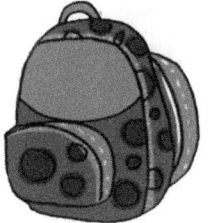 ?

Measure

99

Lesson 2: **Using balance scales to compare weight**

• Compare the weight of objects using balance scales

Challenge 1

1 Draw something lighter.

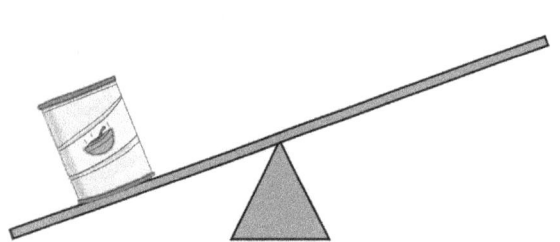

2 Draw something heavier.

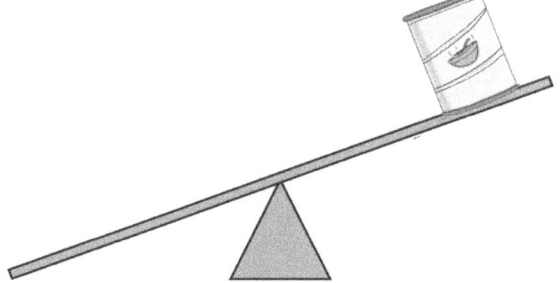

Challenge 2

Draw a line from each animal to its correct place on the balance scales.

1

2

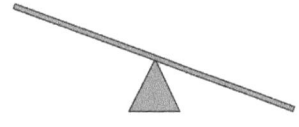

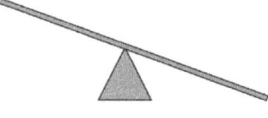

Challenge 3

Circle the word that is true for the square.

1

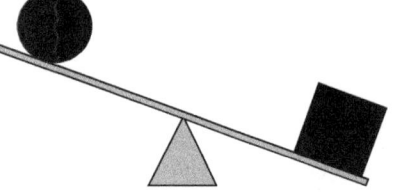

heavier   lighter   same

2

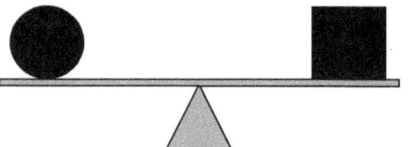

heavier   lighter   same

Lesson 3: **Estimating and ordering objects by weight**

- Order objects from heaviest to lightest or lightest to heaviest

Challenge 1 Draw the fruit in order from lightest to heaviest.

lightest		heaviest

Challenge 2 Draw something lighter and heavier.

lighter	heavier

Challenge 3 Choose four objects and estimate the order.
Draw them in the boxes.

heaviest			lightest

101

Lesson 4: **Measuring weight**

Measure

• Weigh objects using units that are the same

Challenge 1   How many cubes?

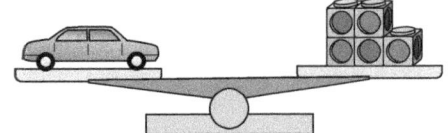

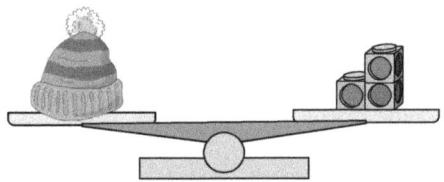

1 The toy car weighs
☐ cubes.

2 The hat weighs
☐ cubes.

Challenge 2   Add or take away cubes to make the scale balance.

1

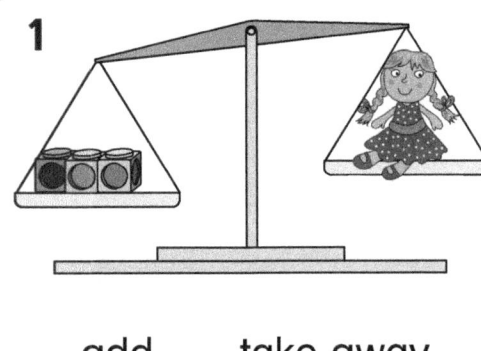

2

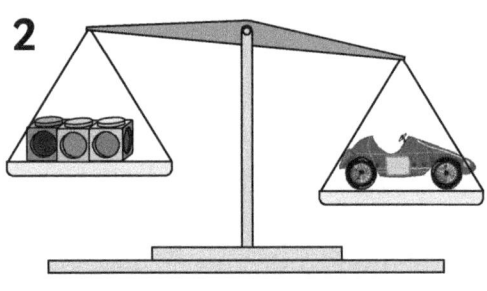

add   take away

add   take away

Challenge 3

 = 3 cubes   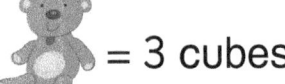 = 2 cubes   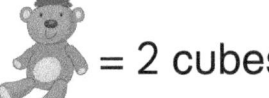 = 1 cube

1 The 3 bears weigh ☐ cubes.

2 Draw cubes on the scale to make it balance.

Lesson 1: **Comparing and describing capacity**

- Recognise when a container is full, half full and empty

You will need
- blue coloured pencil

 Colour the glass until it is full.

 Colour to make the labels true.

empty   full   half full

Draw a line to the correct label.

  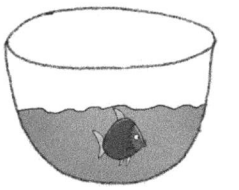   

empty   full   half full

Lesson 2: **Estimating and ordering capacity**

- Estimate and order capacity from most to least and from least to most

Challenge 1 Circle the container that holds the most.

Challenge 2 Order the capacities from holds the least (1) to holds the most (4).

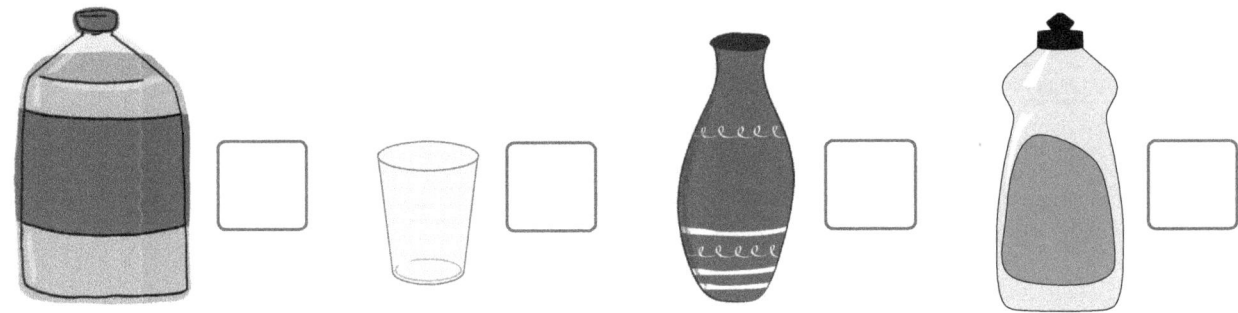

Challenge 3 Draw the containers from Challenge 2 in order, from holds the most to holds the least.

Lesson 3: **Measuring capacities**

- Measure capacity using units of measurement that are the same

You will need
- toy bucket
- jug
- yoghurt pots

Measure

Challenge 1

Fill the jug with water using the yoghurt pot.

The capacity of the jug is ☐ yoghurt pots.

Challenge 2

Fill the bucket with water using the jug. How many jugs did you need to fill the bucket?

Draw them:

Challenge 3

Which is the best container to use to fill the paddling pool? Circle it.

Lesson 4: **Estimating and measuring capacities**

- Estimate a capacity, measure it and describe the results

You will need
- measuring jug
- cups
- bucket
- spread tubs/yoghurt pots

Challenge 1 Which container is best for filling the bucket? Circle it.

Challenge 2 Measure to check this estimate.

Container	Estimate	Measure

Challenge 3 Fill in your estimate then measure to check it.

Container	Estimate	Measure

Lesson 1: **Recognising times of the day**

• Recognise morning, afternoon, day and night and learn what takes a minute and an hour

 Circle the correct time of day for these activities.

1

day   night

2

day   night

3

day   night

 Circle how long it takes to do each activity.

1 Go up and down the slide

minutes   hours

2 Brush your teeth

minutes   hours

3 Do your homework

minutes   hours

 How long? Draw a line to the right time.

wave   sleep   sneeze

less than a minute   more than an hour

107

Lesson 2: **Reading the time**

• Read the time to the hour

Challenge 1 Circle the right time.

1

2

3

5 o'clock 8 o'clock   12 o'clock 3 o'clock   11 o'clock 1 o'clock

Challenge 2 Write the time each clock shows.

1 _____ **2** _____ **3** _____

Challenge 3
  1 Fill in the numbers.
  2 Set the time to 4 o'clock.

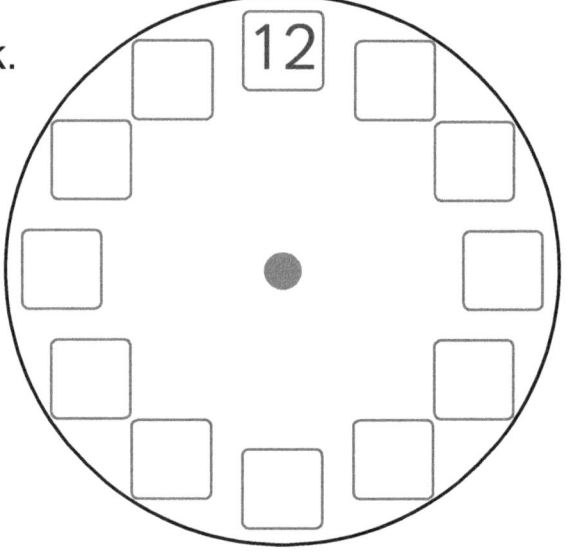

Lesson 3: **Showing the time**

• Show the time to the hour

Measure

Challenge 1 Draw the hour hand on each clock.

1

4:00

2

11:00

3

8:00

Challenge 2 Show the times on the clocks.

1
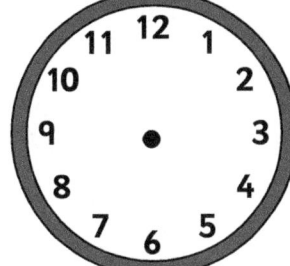

10 o'clock

2

12 o'clock

3
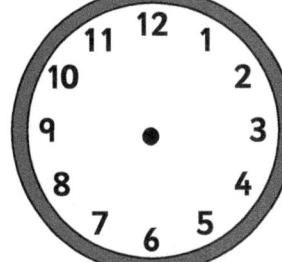

1 o'clock

Challenge 3 A film starts a 3 o'clock and is 2 hours long.
Show the finishing time on the blank clock.

Start time

Finishing time

109

Lesson 4: **Recognising and ordering times of day**

• Order my day using times on the hour

Measure

Challenge 1 Put the events in order: first, second, third, fourth.

Challenge 2 Show the times on the clocks.

1 Wake up in the morning.

_____

2 Eat lunch.

_____

3 Go home from school.

_____

4 Go to bed at night.

_____

Challenge 3 Draw something you do after school. Show the time on the clock.

Lesson 1: **Days of the week**

- Recognise the days of the week

Challenge 1 Draw a weekday activity.

You will need
- red and blue coloured pencils

Challenge 2 Weekend, weekday or both?

Activity	Weekend	Weekday	Both

Challenge 3 Colour the weekend days red and the weekdays blue.

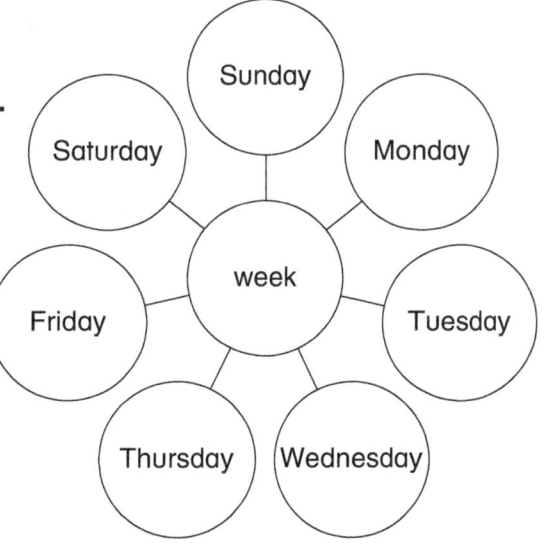

111

Lesson 2: **Ordering the days of the week**

• Order the days of the week

Challenge 1 Draw lines to put the days of the week in order.

Wednesday   Monday   Sunday   Thursday   Friday

| | Tuesday | | | | | Saturday | |

Challenge 2 Write the day that comes next.

1 Tuesday, Wednesday,

2 Saturday, Sunday,

3 Wednesday, Thursday,

Challenge 3 Write the day before and the day after.

Yesterday	Today	Tomorrow
	Monday	
	Friday	
	Wednesday	

Lesson 3: **Ordering familiar events**

• Order events by days of the week

Challenge 1 Order the routine 1, 2, 3, 4.

Challenge 2 Order the activity with numbers 1, 2, 3, 4.

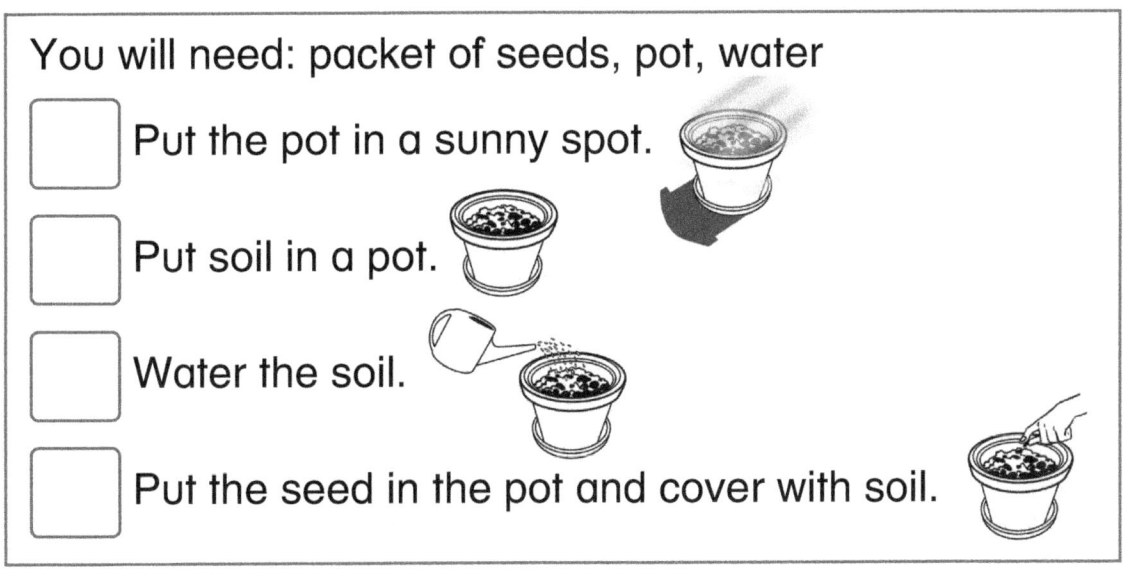

You will need: packet of seeds, pot, water

Put the pot in a sunny spot.

Put soil in a pot.

Water the soil.

Put the seed in the pot and cover with soil.

Challenge 3 Draw your first two activities on a Monday.

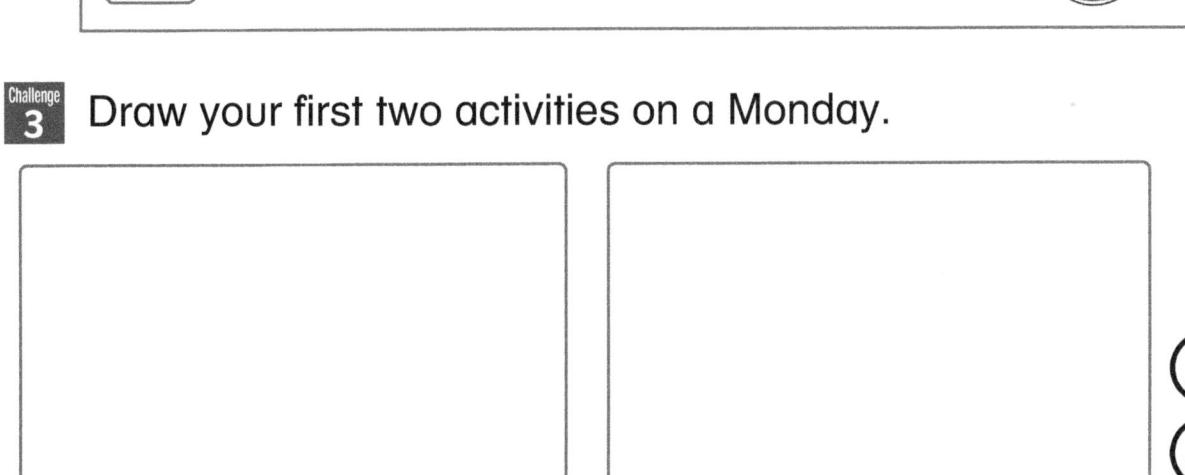

113

Lesson 4: **Months of the year**

• Recognise and order the months of the year

Challenge 1 Draw an event that happens every year.

Challenge 2 Write the months in order.

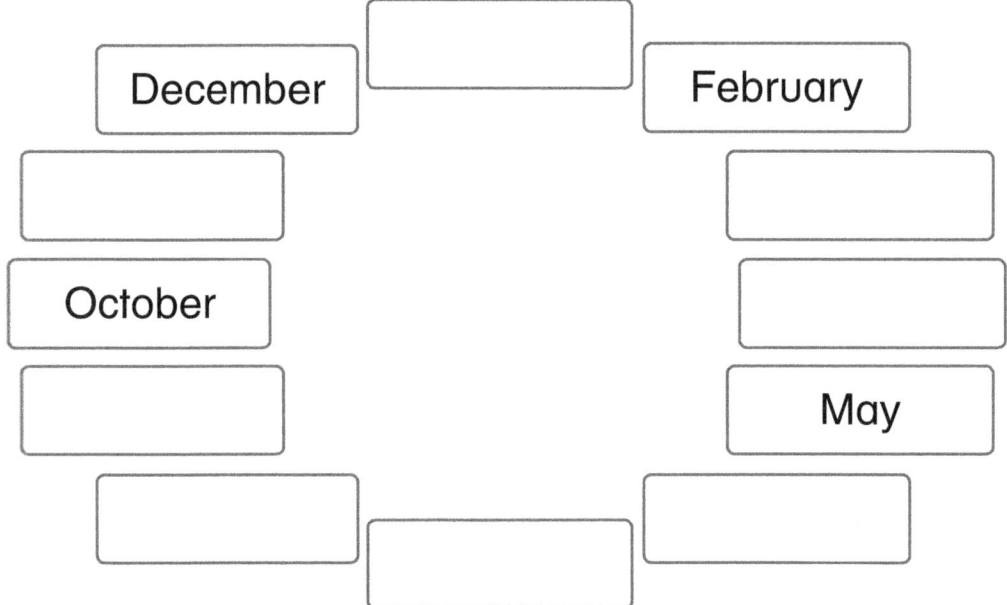

December

February

October

May

Challenge 3 **1** Write the name of the missing season.

2 Draw the weather for that season in the box.

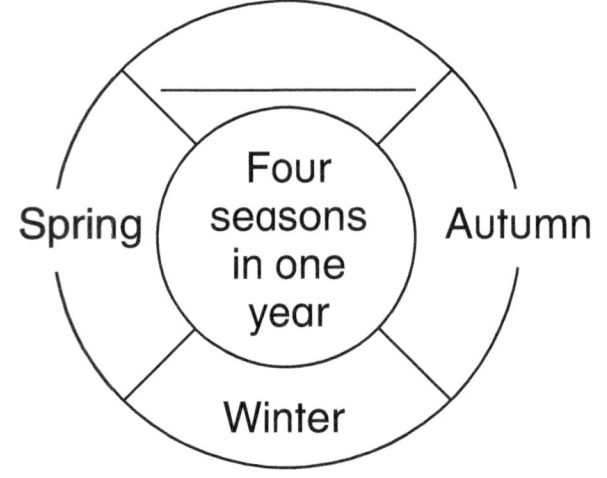

Spring

Four
seasons
in one
year

Autumn

Winter

• Sort information to answer questions

Challenge 1 Draw a line to the right answer.

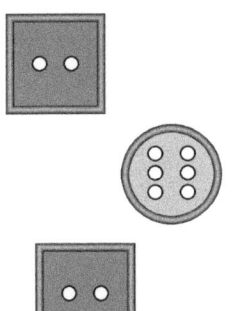

round

square

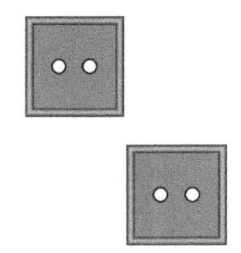

Challenge 2 Draw a line to the right answer.

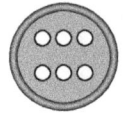  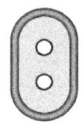   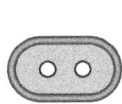  

2 holes

6 holes

Challenge 3 Write the letters and numbers in the correct box.

Letters	Numbers

A 3 B J 5 10 T 9

K P 6 N W 4 L 7

Handling data

- Organise information into lists and tables

You will need
- different coloured pencils

Challenge 1 Complete the table.

Sweet	Total

Challenge 2 Complete the table.

Vehicle	Total

Challenge 3 Complete the table.

Button type	Total

Lesson 3: **Pictograms**

• Use a pictogram to show information

Challenge 1 Write the totals.

Cakes sold		Total
Monday		
Tuesday		
Wednesday		

Challenge 2 Write the totals.

Safari park		Total
giraffe		
zebra		
tiger		
wolf		
bear		

Challenge 3 Use the table to complete the pictogram.

Type of groceries	Number of items
banana	2
apple	5
popcorn	3
water	3

Supermarket sales

banana	
apple	
popcorn	
water	

Handling data

• Use a block graph to show information

You will need
• coloured pencils

Challenge 1

Complete the block graph.

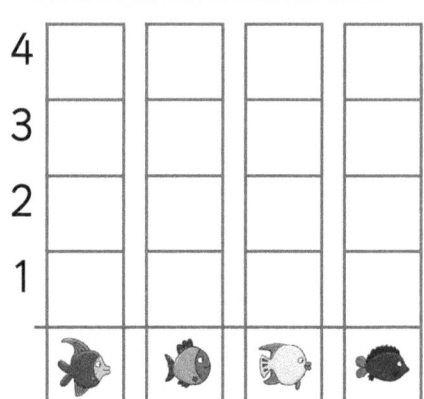

Challenge 2

Use the table to draw a block graph. Use blue to colour the column with the most.

🍅	7
🍄	5
🥕	9
🌽	6

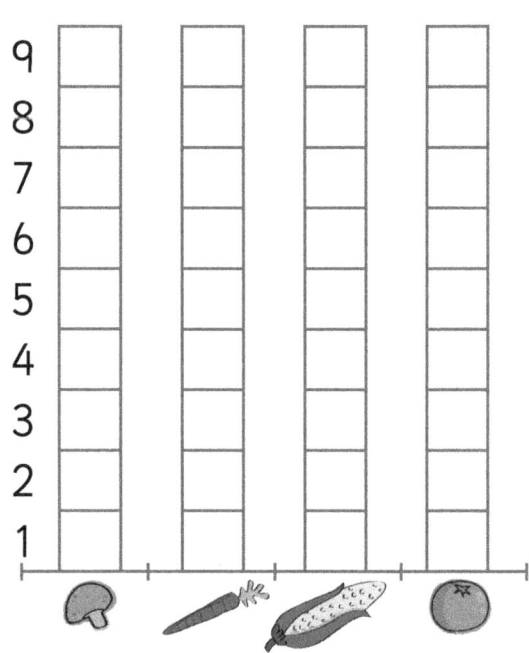

Challenge 3

Complete the block graph.

red
8

blue
10

green
5

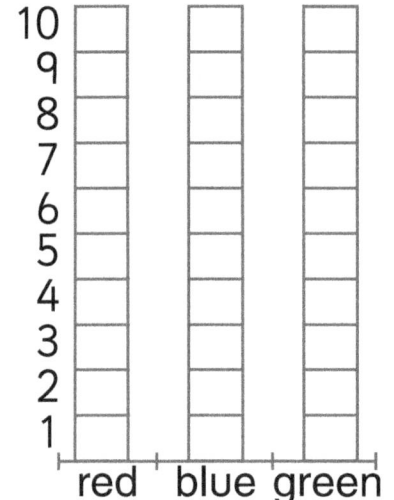

red   blue   green

Lesson 1: **Venn diagrams**

- Use a Venn diagram to sort information

Challenge 1 Write the numbers in the diagram.

4, 10, 21, 25, 28, 24, 29.

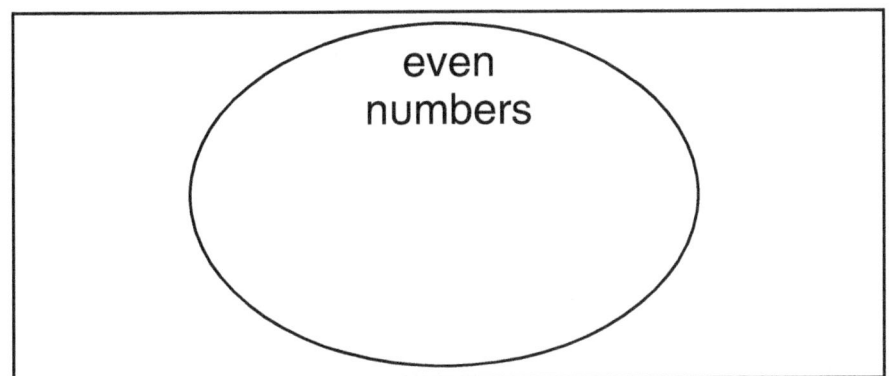

even numbers

Challenge 2 Complete the Venn diagram.

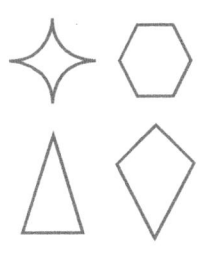

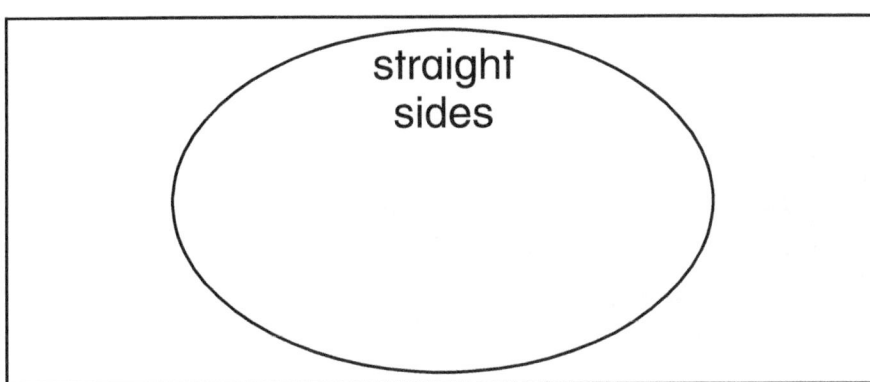

straight sides

Challenge 3 Complete the label.

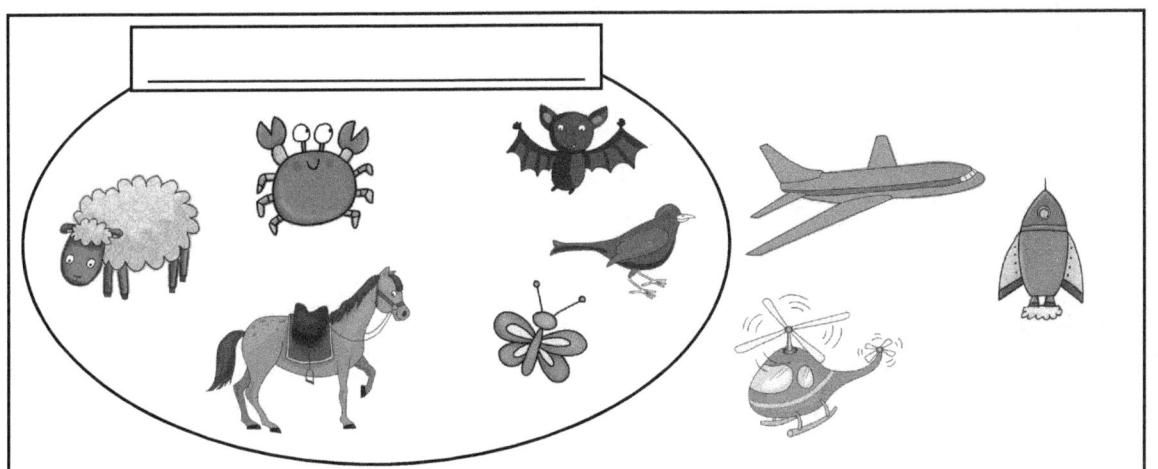

Handling data

Lesson 2: **Carroll diagrams**

• Use a Carroll diagram to sort information

Challenge 1 Complete the Carroll diagram.

A B C
D E

Letters with curves	Letters with no curves

Challenge 2 Draw a line to show where each animal belongs.

Lives in water	Does not live in water

Challenge 3 Complete the diagram.

Less than 10	More than 10

• Collect and sort information to answer a question

Challenge 1 Complete the tally chart.

Vehicle	Number
lorries	
cars	
motorbikes	

Challenge 2 Complete the table.

Vehicle	Number	Total
lorries	ＨＨ ＨＨＩＩＩＩ	
cars	ＨＨ ＨＨ ＨＨ ＨＨＩＩＩ	
motorbikes		11
taxis	ＨＨ	

How many?

1  [   ]   2  [   ]

Challenge 3 Use the information in the table above to answer the questions.

1 How many more lorries than taxis? [   ]

2 How many more cars than motorbikes? [   ]

3 How many vehicles in total? [   ]

121

Lesson 4: **Collecting, sorting and presenting data**

Handling data

• Collect, sort and present information

Challenge 1 Use the information to complete a pictogram.

Fruit	Number
🍎	3
🍌	5
🍎	8
🍐	2
🍒	1

Favourite fruit

🍎	☺ ☺ ☺
🍌	
🍎	
🍐	
🍒	

Challenge 2 Use the information to draw a block graph.

Challenge 3 Use the information to answer the questions.

1 How many people like  ? _____

2 How many people like  ? _____

3 How many people were asked? _____

Notes

Notes